Speaking Freely

LANDMARK LAW CASES & AMERICAN SOCIETY

Peter Charles Hoffer
N. E. H. Hull
Series Editors

For a complete list of titles in the series go to www.kansaspress.ku.edu

PHILIPPA STRUM

Speaking Freely

Whitney v. California

and American Speech Law

UNIVERSITY PRESS OF KANSAS

Published by the University Press of Kansas (Lawrence, Kansas 66045), which was organized by the Kansas Board of Regents and is operated and funded by Emporia State University, Fort Hays State University, Kansas State University, Pittsburg State University, the University of Kansas, and Wichita State University

Library of Congress Cataloging-in-Publication Data

Strum, Philippa, author.
Speaking freely : Whitney v. California and American speech law / Philippa Strum.
pages cm — (Landmark law cases and American society)
Includes bibliographical references and index.
ISBN 978-0-7006-2134-7 (hardback)
ISBN 978-0-7006-2135-4 (paperback)
ISBN 978-0-7006-2167-5 (ebook)
1. Whitney, Anita, 1867–1955—Trials, litigation, etc. 2. Freedom of speech—United States—Cases. 3. Criminal syndicalism—United States—Cases. I. Title.
KF224.W543S777 2015
342.7308'53—dc23
2015023668

British Library Cataloguing-in-Publication Data is available.

Printed in the United States of America

10 9 8 7 6 5 4 3 2 1

The paper used in this publication is recycled and contains 30 percent postconsumer waste. It is acid free and meets the minimum requirements of the American National Standard for Permanence of Paper for Printed Library Materials Z39.48-1992.

For
Alexa Lauren Weiss
and her parents
Terra Weiss
David Strum Weiss

CONTENTS

"Who can find a virtuous woman? For her price is above rubies." Surely Anita Whitney fit this description. Born into privilege and wealth, she worked for the betterment of the downtrodden. In a time of reaction, she championed reform. Never physically imposing, she withstood the weight of unfair accusations and partial justice. Indicted for the crime of speaking truth to power, she lost her law cases but not her cause.

Now almost forgotten, Whitney's role in the campaign for a robust First Amendment has found a worthy champion. Philippa Strum, a senior scholar at the Woodrow Wilson International Center for Scholars, brings to *Whitney v. California* the well-honed skills of a legal historian and the insight of a biographer. Mining biographical materials, trial records, newspaper accounts, and legal papers, Strum follows the triumphs and travails of the Whitney case through the Progressive Era, into the I.W.W., California politics, and the state and federal courts. The result is a moving and brilliant essay.

If there is a hero in the story to match Whitney's heroism, it is Louis D. Brandeis. To some extent his career and beliefs followed hers, although paths to power were open to him that long-held prejudices denied to her. He understood the importance of her free speech claims and penned the language that would make them part of American law. Strum has written about Brandeis in a variety of contexts. Here she brings him into the tale in just the right place and reveals his part in it.

Speaking Freely is Philippa Strum's third book in the Landmark Law Cases and American Society series. Along with her *When the Nazis Came to Skokie* and *Mendez v. Westminster* it sparkles with her commitment to the highest aspirations of the law and the finest standards of historical craft. No one will come away from *Speaking Freely* unmoved by Whitney's courage, Brandeis's idealism, and Strum's narrative.

ACKNOWLEDGMENTS

Anita Whitney was a committed communist, so she would be the first to acknowledge that most undertakings are communal in one way or another. That certainly is true of a book. My heartfelt thanks go to the many people who made this one possible, with the usual disclaimer that I, not they, am responsible for the final product and whatever flaws it may have.

Vincent Blasi, John Ferren, H. N. Hirsch, Jill Norgren, Peter Rajsingh, and Melvin Urofsky read complete drafts of one iteration or another of the manuscript. Jill, whose eagle eye and insight I have relied on for decades, read some chapters more than once.

Members of the Red Line Group, an extraordinary collection of Woodrow Wilson International Center for Scholars alumni, read each chapter as it was drafted. Their feedback throughout the process was crucial. Thank you Marie-Therese Connolly, Mary Ellen Curtin, Matt Dallek, Robyn Muncy, and Wendy Williams, for your endless support and your treasured friendship.

Eric Arnesen and Douglas Reed read and commented on early drafts of the chapter on labor; David Cole, the chapters on the trial. Daniel Kohrman, Terra Weiss, and Zipporah Wiseman all worked their way through one or more chapters. So did Siya Hegde, my research assistant during the last stages of the book, who also found obscure materials that I needed and with a discerning eagle eye read over everything I wrote. She and I both built on the impressive work of Aislin Kavaldjian, the research assistant who preceded her.

They and I could not have uncovered as much as we did without the wonderfully knowledgeable and persistent librarians at the Wilson Center: Janet Spikes, Michelle Kamelich, and Katherine Wahler. Michelle was especially adept at locating hard-to-find materials at libraries around the country and negotiating for their use.

Thanks go to the people at those libraries and others, particularly Emily Foster and Jeanne V. Diller, of the Oakland Public Library; Kathleen M. Sheehan, of the Harvard University Archives; Amanda M. Pike, of the Seeley G. Mudd Manuscript Library at Princeton University; Lea Jordan, of the Manuscripts and Archives Division at the New York

Public Library; Roslyn Pachoca and Lewis Wyman, at the Library of Congress; and various librarians at the Bancroft Library of the University of California-Berkeley and the California State Library at Sacramento. I am grateful as well to Alison Arman, who scoured the Neylan papers for me; to Eric Kay, for research on the use of Justice Brandeis's *Whitney* opinion; to Meg Gale, for help deciphering the mysteries of the California code; and to Don Wolfensberger, for his guidance to all things congressional.

A special note of gratitude goes to Supreme Court Justice Ruth Bader Ginsburg and to Cathy Vaughan, her assistant sans pareil, who made the Supreme Court's file on the Whitney case available to me. The Superior Court in Alameda, where Anita Whitney was tried, has been unable to locate the trial record, and so I could not have written this book without the help of Justice Ginsburg and Ms. Vaughan.

The Woodrow Wilson International Center for Scholars has been my scholarly home since 2001. It provides the best venue I can imagine for any scholar: physical space, the amazing librarians and research assistants mentioned earlier, an endlessly helpful IT staff, and a community of colleagues. What is perhaps best of all, as any academic will understand, there are no committee meetings and no exams to grade. I could not be more grateful for my inclusion in that community.

Finally, thanks to the staff of the University Press of Kansas, which has been supportive through so many of my books and continues to be a pleasure to work with: Michael Briggs, Charles Myers, Larisa Martin, Michael Kehoe, and Rebecca Murray.

This book is dedicated to Alexa Lauren Weiss, my granddaughter, who at an early age is already making full use of her speech rights. I trust she will continue to do so when she is old enough to participate in the political process beyond helping her father indicate his favored candidates in the voting booth. It is dedicated as well to her parents, David Strum Weiss and Terra Weiss, for their nonstop encouragement while I worked on the book. I'm not sure they will ever see what they insist should be the movie version of the *Whitney* story, but I hope that in the meantime they, and other readers, will enjoy this one.

Speaking Freely

Introduction

Americans take the right to speech for granted. The Internet, airwaves, auditoriums, college campuses, and many other venues are filled with political commentary, much of it far from laudatory. Officeholders and the government itself are criticized as frequently as they are praised, sometimes without much basis in fact and in language that is anything but restrained. And yet no one is put on trial for the kind of speech that would lead to arrest in many other nations.

Most Americans do not realize that this was not always true. In the early twentieth century, both Congress and almost half of the nation's states enacted laws that severely circumscribed Americans' right to speak. Thousands of Americans were prosecuted for speech that was critical of the government, and many were jailed.

One of them was a California woman named Charlotte Anita Whitney. In 1920 the state of California put her on trial, and in 1927 the United States Supreme Court upheld her conviction for helping to organize a political party that called for sweeping changes in the American political and economic systems. Yet the opinion that Justice Louis Dembitz Brandeis wrote in the case of *Whitney v. California* soon led to the United States' uniquely permissive approach to speech. That was somewhat surprising, as Brandeis had earlier voted repeatedly to uphold laws restricting speech.

The discussion of *Whitney v. California* that follows is therefore an exploration not only of *how* American speech law became what it is today but of *why* the United States gives such free rein to speech. It is also a study of the way law and society interact and of the impact that institutions and personalities have on one another.

CHAPTER ONE

From Silver Spoon to Socialism

When Charlotte Anita Whitney became a Communist in 1919, she thought she was following in the footsteps of the Puritans who had helped create the United States. The state of California saw it a bit differently, and put her in jail.

Whitney v. California is the story of an American aristocrat who developed into both a twentieth-century radical and a flashpoint for the creation of modern American speech jurisprudence, which remains more liberal than that of any other nation in the world. It is a tale that brings together early-twentieth-century settlement houses in the teeming immigrant neighborhoods of the eastern United States, the turbulent strikes of the Industrial Workers of the World in both the East and the West, the American approach to domestic security during World War I, and a son of immigrants who became one of the nation's most influential Supreme Court justices.

We may think of law as a matter of courts and judges and doctrines, but it begins as the story of human beings and their attempts to make sense of and organize their world. Whitney's journey from a cosseted descendant of Pilgrims to a convicted criminal reflects her effort to understand why justice had not been achieved in an industrializing society, and to do something about it. It resulted in a landmark opinion in the 1927 case of *Whitney v. California* and a dramatic alteration of the United States' definition of free speech—one that is repeated in courtrooms throughout the country to this day.

Whitney was sent to jail in the twentieth century, but her story begins in the nineteenth century and even, in a sense, in the seventeenth. By the time Anita Whitney, as she was usually known, was born in 1867, her ancestors had been in the New World for more than 200 years. Five of her father's forebears reportedly arrived on the Mayflower in 1620; others, only a few years later. One of them was Thomas Dudley, the second governor of the Massachusetts Bay Colony and a founder of Harvard College (later Harvard University). His son Joseph followed in his father's footsteps by becoming governor of Massachusetts and New Hampshire. Harvard's Dudley House is named for the family. The family of Mary Field Whitney, Anita Whitney's mother, arrived in Maryland in 1640. Whitneys and Fields were officers in George Washington's army during the American Revolution. Their descendants continued on distinguished paths as the next centuries unfolded. Cyrus W. Field, another ancestor, was responsible for creating the first transatlantic telegraph cable, in 1858; Whitney's cousin Dudley Field Malone would become an assistant secretary of state under Woodrow Wilson and a lawyer for suffragists. One of her aunts was married to Supreme Court Justice Stephen Field, appointed to the bench by Abraham Lincoln. Anita spent much of her childhood, her college Christmas vacations, and two of her early teen years with Justice Field and his wife in Washington. She was such a favorite that the childless Field left one-third of his estate to her. Anita's father, George Edwin Whitney, had moved to California from New England before she was born and became Alameda County's representative in the state senate. Hers was a family that read the Declaration of Independence out loud on every Fourth of July. To them, the Declaration was not simply part of the American story; it was a piece of their own family history.

Anita, the second of seven children, was born in Oakland, California, just two years after the end of the Civil War. During her childhood the South was going through the Reconstruction Era, and the industrialization of the North was just beginning. It was a tumultuous time for the nation, and both the emphasis on African Americans' rights and the results of industrialization would become important to Whitney. But that came later; in her early years, like any other child, she was focused on family and the education she got in California schools. After Whitney finished high school her parents sent her east to Wellesley College, in the state her father's ancestors had helped create. He wanted her to appreciate the part of the country that had forged both its government and its literature. Arriving at Wellesley in 1885, Whitney became one of the less than 2 percent of all American women who went on to higher education in the 1880s. The majority of them were, like Whitney, from privileged homes. She would always remember Wellesley, where the students were required to attend chapel every day, as a place of welcome spirituality. On school holidays she was an enthusiastic visitor to American revolutionary sites in Boston, Concord, and Lexington. She read Ralph Waldo Emerson, James Russell Lowell, and Henry David Thoreau, all of whom celebrated quintessentially American values. She wrote that she gloried in being "American clear through to my very marrow . . . I was glad of my colonial ancestry and proud that the roots of my family were planted deep in American soil." Whitney never lost the sense that she was one of the torchbearers of the original flame of American principles.

She graduated from Wellesley in 1889, and then departed on the months-long tour of Europe that was frequently bestowed on wealthy college graduates by their indulgent parents.

After that Whitney floundered. She briefly taught Sunday school in Oakland—her family was solidly Episcopalian as well as Republican—and participated in college alumnae activities. None of that satisfied her. "I was always more or less conscious of a feeling of boredom," she would say later, "coupled with a dread of being thought different." She was, however, about to become very different.

In 1893, Whitney went to a class reunion at Wellesley. Curious about what some of her classmates had told her they were doing, she followed them to New York City to see the College Settlement House where they were working. It was Whitney's first glimpse of immigrants, and of poverty.

The settlement house movement in the United States dated from at least as early as 1889, when Jane Addams and some friends opened Hull House in Chicago. Settlement houses, staffed primarily by young unmarried women college graduates, soon appeared elsewhere in the overflowing neighborhoods populated by new arrivals in the United States. The urban tenement dwellers, trapped in low-paying jobs for ten- and twelve-hour days or at home with ill-clad children who lacked access to adequate food and even rudimentary health services, could expect little or nothing from government in the way of help. Settlement houses, where the volunteers lived and worked, tried to fill at least some of the gap.

That was the mission of the College Settlement House, which occupied an old renovated building in a crowded immigrant neighborhood on Manhattan's Lower East Side. The college-educated women who lived and worked in it sought out people from the neighborhood, organized activities for and with them, and took what comfort they could offer into the immigrants' impoverished homes. Other privileged New York women occasionally volunteered at the settlement house. A young Eleanor Roosevelt was one of them, taking the streetcar from the elegant Upper East Side in order to teach children calisthenics and dancing, and occasionally bringing her cousin Franklin Delano Roosevelt to see her work.

There were nonetheless never enough volunteers for all the work that needed to be done, so Whitney began helping out during what was planned as a one-week stay. Her ventures into tenements during her week's visit terrified her because of what she described as their "sickeningly odorous" dampness, rickety staircases, and poor ventilation. The tenements were filled with "the fumes of the accumulated life of so many people," Whitney would write, and the cockroaches seemed as much at home there as the impoverished humans. Nonetheless, at the end of the week, she accepted an invitation to join the staff. "The revelation of the conditions under which a really good worker had to live in New York hit me with sickening force," she reported. She was appalled that "some cog in our social system had slipped. . . . I wanted to help change it. Here at last was something vital to be done." She helped in the library, took soup to the sick, and visited the elderly. She also taught sewing and cooking, going to a cooking school herself in the mornings so she could learn what to teach her club of girls in the evening.

Whitney stayed at College Settlement House for only a few months, however, before being called home to Oakland. Her father was terminally ill. After his death Whitney moved in with her widowed mother and began to work as a teacher in private schools while she read what she could find about poverty and tenements. "If everyone knows about these things, why do they go on?" she would recall wondering. "Is human life then so cheap?" She was shocked to read that some of what she called "the oldest and vilest New York tenements" were profitably owned by the Trinity Church. That led her to ponder the relationship between respected American institutions and the kind of poverty she had seen in New York. Eager to do what she could, she organized a club for boys and girls in a slum district of West Oakland, and joined the council of the Associated Charities of Alameda County.

In 1901, when she was 34 years old, Whitney left teaching to become the Associated Charities' secretary. Her salary was $85 a month, and a colleague remembered Whitney economizing by eating little while she gave away what money she had to people in need. Speaking of those she helped, she later said, "I loved my people. I entered into human relationships I had not known before." She was particularly concerned about juvenile delinquents, certain that with the proper help they could be turned away from crime, and she lobbied for the creation of juvenile courts and housing for juvenile delinquents separate from that of adults. When California created a juvenile court system in 1903, Whitney became the first—unpaid—juvenile probation officer in Alameda County, and was frequently given temporary custody of children in trouble. The position became a paid one later on, and at that point Whitney was replaced by a man.

By the time that happened, Whitney had begun to wonder whether it was possible that "no real solution [to poverty] lay along the route of organized charities." Thinking that perhaps her dissatisfaction with the limited impact of charities meant that she just wasn't going about charitable work the right way, she gave up her job with Associated Charities in 1907 and went to New York and Boston to work with more experienced social workers. Her goal was to see if they were making a real difference. The journey left her disenchanted. Horrified as she was by New York tenements, she was even more distressed by the rampant and seemingly intractable alcoholism she found in the slums of East Boston. "What impressed me most during those days," she recalled, "was the indifference of the well to do. It seemed almost incredible that people who had everything can be absolutely so unresponsible [*sic*] to the needs of others." Her growing sense of futility confused her. She returned to California but "abandoned the profession that I had hoped was to be my life work" in 1911, finding herself "left adrift again with more questions to be answered."

A period of depression followed, as Whitney tried to rethink the direction of her life. For a while, reacting to her experiences in Boston, she became involved with the prohibition movement. Soon, however, she found a new cause. It was woman suffrage.

She joined California's Woman Suffrage Party, the Club-Women's Franchise League, and the Equal Suffrage League of San Francisco. Working tirelessly, as seemed to have been her wont in any cause she espoused, she became president of the College Equal Suffrage League of California. The movement of which it was a part succeeded: in October 1911 an amendment to the California constitution giving women the vote was ratified. Whitney promptly took her suffrage work onto a national stage, becoming second vice president of the National American Woman Suffrage Association (Jane Addams was its first vice president) and journeying to Oregon and Nevada between 1911 and 1914 to work in those states' suffrage efforts. Returning to California, Whitney helped the College Equal Suffrage League reorganize itself as the California Civic League and became its president. She joined the board of the new Society for Abolition of the Death Penalty in California and organized a San Francisco branch of Travelers Aid to ensure the safety of young women arriving to seek work during the 1915 world's fair, formally the Panama Pacific International Exposition. All the while, she lobbied in Sacramento, California's capital, for women's right to sit on juries—a fight that was won in 1917—and for minimum wages for women and children, pasteurization of milk, the elimination of red-light districts, and mandatory physical education in public schools.

At that point, Whitney was following the path of a good Progressive. Her activities reflected the Progressives' belief that the federal and state governments as constituted could alleviate the plight of disadvantaged Americans and make life better for all the nation's people. Unlike most Progressives, however, Whitney was inching toward the labor movement in a way that would ultimately lead her to adopt a much more radical ideology.

Back in 1906, when a huge earthquake and fire ravaged San Francisco, the efficient Whitney had helped organize camps in San Francisco and Oakland for displaced residents. She noticed that labor unions were particularly useful in finding employment for refugees from the city. She had already encountered unionists of the Women's Trade Union Label League and the Wage Earners League—as well as Socialists, and that would become important later on—while working for suffrage and lobbying in Sacramento. She heard and was impressed by Eugene Victor Debs, the Socialist candidate for president, while she was doing suffrage work in Oregon. When thousands of textile workers struck for better working conditions in Lawrence, Massachusetts, in 1912 and Paterson, New Jersey, in 1913, some of their leaders spoke in California, and Whitney listened carefully to their insistence that only unions could better the lives of laborers.

The union leaders she heard, however, were not mainstream labor organizers. The nation's largest workers' organization was the American Federation of Labor (AFL), which sought to bring together skilled workers in one particular specialization—carpenters, for example, or blast furnace workers or garment cutters—in a craft union. It focused on fighting for better wages and working conditions within the existing economic system. That was not the approach of the speakers from Lawrence and Paterson, like Elizabeth Gurley Flynn, Arturo Giovannitti, and William ("Big Bill") Haywood, who excited Whitney. They came instead from the Industrial Workers of the World (I.W.W.), and in not too many years Anita Whitney would in effect be jailed for sympathizing with them.

The I.W.W., familiarly known as the Wobblies, was organized in Chicago in 1905. Its goal was first to bring all workers in a workplace and an industry—skilled, unskilled, men, women—into a union, and then to merge all the workers across the country into what it called the One Big Union. Eventually, the I.W.W. believed, the unified laborers would go out on a nationwide general strike that would force the capitalists to turn industry over to the workers. The Wobblies scorned the American Federation of Labor for its exclusion of the racial minorities, noncitizen immigrants, and unskilled laborers who made up an increasing share of the wage-earning population. They envisioned a society without child labor, unemployment, or inequality of the sexes—as well as without a government, which they thought could in some unspecified fashion be replaced by groups of experts.

They rejected the AFL's emphasis on craft unions, believing that such unions isolated workers within a workplace when what was needed was unity across specializations. They disagreed as well with the traditional unions' assumption that labor could achieve power and a decent standard of living under the capitalist system. Where the AFL would, for example, organize carpenters, electricians, and bricklayers into separate trade unions, the Wobblies would bring them together into an overall union of construction workers. They would fight for decent wages and working conditions as a temporary palliative, but their vision of the future was one without capitalism. Drawing on Marxist rhetoric, the Wobblies envisioned workers as cohering because they were members of a class that was inexorably opposed to the other, "capitalist" class. "The working class and the employing class have nothing in common," the I.W.W. constitution proclaimed.

> Between these two classes a struggle must go on until the workers of the world organize as a class, take possession of the means of production, abolish the wage system, and live in harmony with the Earth. . . . It is the historic mission of the working class to do away with capitalism. The army of production must be organized, not only for everyday struggle with capitalists, but also to carry on production when capitalism shall have been overthrown. By organizing industrially we are forming the structure of the new society within the shell of the old.

Many of the Wobblies were migratory workers who moved, variously, among farms, construction sites, coal mines, and timber camps. They formed an industrial underclass of societally disinherited people who viewed the existing social and economic structure as promising nothing at all for them beyond lives of overly long labor, starvation wages, and subhuman working conditions. They were precisely the kinds of people Karl Marx could have had in mind when he wrote that workers who rebelled had nothing to lose but their chains, and they acted accordingly. The I.W.W. declared itself to be "revolutionary," and from the time of its first convention its radical rhetoric could not have been better designed to frighten both employers and the average American citizen. According to the minutes of the founding convention, the delegates cheered labor firebrand Big Bill Haywood when he declared, "The aims and objects of this organization should be to put the working class in possession of the economic power, the means of life, in control of the machinery of production and distribution, without regard to capitalist masters."

The Wobblies soon produced a *Little Red Song Book* that contained lyrics such as "Come on, you fellows, get in line; we'll fill the boss with fears; Red's the color of our flag, it's stained with blood and tears . . . when we hit their pocketbooks we'll spoil their smiles of mirth—We'll stop their dirty dividends and drive them from the earth with One Big Industrial Union!" Another song called for sabotage:

> I had a job once threshing wheat, worked sixteen hours with hands and feet . . .
> One moonlight night, I hate to tell, I "accidentally" slipped and fell,
> My pitchfork went right in between some cog wheels on that thresh machine . . .
> Next day that stingy rube did say . . .
> "You grease my wagon up, you mutt, and don't forget to screw the nut."
> I greased his wagon all right, but I plumb forgot to screw the nut,
> And when he started on that trip, the wheels slipped off and broke his hip.

The songs would be introduced as evidence when the state of California put Anita Whitney on trial. So would I.W.W. publications that declared, "Direct action, sabotage, passive resistance, intermittent and irritation strikes are some of the tactics of the revolutionary Industrial Workers of the World. . . . These skirmishes are the prelude to the social general strike that will end the rule of the capitalist and abolish economic classes from human society." Although the Wobblies frequently emphasized nonviolence and passive resistance, much of their language was far less restrained than the actions some of them actually took, and at times they sent mixed messages, making it understandable that the average citizen heard only the rhetoric of violent revolution. Big Bill Haywood could declaim both that "I, for one, have turned my back on violence. . . . We have a new kind of violence—the havoc we raise with money by laying down our tools" and "I despise the law and I am not a law-abiding citizen."

The Wobblies did not merely sing and write, of course; their rhetoric and action went hand in hand. They organized workers in mines, factories, and lumber camps, and backed them up during strikes. One of their great successes came during the Lawrence strike mentioned earlier—a strike that epitomized the conditions that led Whitney to give up on capitalism and the American economy as it was constituted in the first decades of the twentieth century. "The Lawrence and Paterson strikes stirred me to the depths," she wrote. To make sense of the journey Whitney made from a life of privilege to a California jail, it is therefore necessary to understand the negative effects industrialization had on many American workers. The problems were exemplified by life in Lawrence, Massachusetts.

Lawrence was a city of 86,000 people, with some 60,000 of its residents dependent on the textile mills that dominated its economy. The largest mills were owned by the American Woolen Company, a textile trust with mills all across New England. Its workers were primarily immigrants or the children of immigrants: Italians, Poles, Belgians, Eastern European Jews, Russians, Lithuanians, Syrians, Turks. Ray Stannard Baker, the crusading journalist who covered the strike for *The American* magazine and would later become President Woodrow Wilson's press secretary at Versailles, reported that forty-four different languages and dialects were spoken by the workers in Lawrence.

Their working and living conditions were abominable. Baker told his readers that "some of the tenements of Lawrence are the worst I ever saw" and that the workers and their families suffered from "having too little to eat and far too little to wear." According to the U.S. Department of Labor, the cost of food for "an average workingman's family" per year was $422 in 1911; a year later, according to the *New York Times*, it was $466 in states such as Massachusetts. Skilled workers in the Lawrence mills earned between $6 and $10.50 a week; unskilled workers were paid $6 or $7. The rents they were forced to pay were nonetheless as high as those in the far better-off city of New York, Baker wrote, and the food prices were even higher. An unskilled worker earning $7 a week—$364 a year—would not take home enough money to pay for his or her family's food, much less housing, heating, clothing, or medical care. One hundred and seventy-two infants out of every 1,000 born in Lawrence died before their first birthday. Adults also died too young, many of them from the tuberculosis and pneumonia that ran rampant through the tenements. The men, women, and children who survived worked in the mills, and in fact the majority of the workers were women and children—although women and children, thanks to a Massachusetts law, were prohibited from working for more than fifty-six hours a week.

In 1911, the Massachusetts legislature, adopting the mildest of Progressive reforms, voted to reduce the number of hours women and children could work each week to fifty-four. The law took effect at the beginning of 1912, and the reaction of the mill owners to the shortened work week was to cut wages. When workers received their first pay envelopes of the new year on January 11, 1912, they realized that they were being paid less than usual, which they had not anticipated. The difference for the poorly paid workers was the equivalent of several loaves of bread a week, and they walked out on a spontaneous strike. Some of them belonged to the small I.W.W. Lawrence Local 20, but the local's leaders, faced with an uprising they had not planned, quickly realized that they alone could not manage the strike. They sent for help, and I.W.W. leaders such as Joseph Ettor, Big Bill Haywood, and Elizabeth Gurley Flynn rushed to Lawrence.

The local government sympathized with the mill owners, and in response, at Ettor's urging, a crowd of workers marched to the city hall. The mayor called out the police and the militia to deal with the demonstrators and then to patrol the mill district, and what had been a largely peaceful strike turned violent. Fire hoses were turned on strikers picketing the mills; police battled strikers, and a woman died of a bullet wound. Violence was not the strikers' only enemy, however. It was a bitterly cold winter, and even though the I.W.W. organized strike relief, there was not enough food or fuel. The answer was to send some of the strikers' children to New York City, where they could be cared for by sympathetic families until the strike was over. A committee was created to oversee the evacuation. It was directed by Elizabeth Gurley Flynn and Margaret Sanger, the chairman of the Socialist Party's women's committee, who later became famous as a result of her advocacy for birth control. The children were sent by train to Grand Central Station. The journalists covering their arrival told readers about their shock at the sight of the malnourished children, and both the media and angry citizens demanded an investigation.

All the attention led the publicity-conscious mill owners and public officials of Lawrence to declare that no more children could leave the city. When another contingent of children nonetheless arrived at the Lawrence train station to be transported to families in Philadelphia, the police, sent to stop them, waded into the crowd, clubbing mothers and children and throwing them onto military trucks. The horrified journalists were there, too, covering the melee for their readers, and a federal congressional investigation was soon convened.

In March, the mill owners capitulated, raising wages by 5 to 20 percent. The I.W.W. called the strike a success and celebrated its victory. Yet, as Ray Stannard Baker wrote, the settlement meant only that the head of a family who had been earning $6 or $7 a week might get some 10 percent more: "He and his family can live 60 or 70 cents a week better—but consider if you will, how very little 60 or 70 cents a week really means in bread, in rent, in clothing, in fuel, for a family of children." And so, Baker asked, "is not the conclusion forced upon us that changes have got to be different and deeper?"

Anita Whitney was rapidly reaching exactly that conclusion. Her sense that systemic change was needed was heightened when, the following year, the I.W.W. lost a strike in the silk mills of Paterson, New Jersey. There, skilled workers were earning an average of $11.69 a week; unskilled men, $6 or $7; women, an average of $7.17; girls under 16, $1.85. The mill owners managed to crush the strike through a combination of beating and clubbing strikers, arresting hundreds and jailing them in disgusting conditions, closing every hall in Paterson to them, breaking up strike meetings wherever they were held, and confiscating strike literature. Those tactics, along with hunger and the willingness of the elite cadre of skilled workers to sign a separate deal with the mill owners, drove the strikers back to work.

There were also Wobblies much closer to Whitney's home, and the incendiary coverage they were given by California newspapers ensured that she knew about their activities. The I.W.W. had a heavy West Coast component when it was organized and, even before the two East Coast textile strikes, had continued to put much of its energy into the western states. There it became notable for a different kind of action: "free-speech fights."

Like any other union organizers, the Wobblies faced the problem of getting their message out to possible recruits. They were clearly not welcome in the workplaces where their target audience was to be found. They turned instead to speech on the streets, standing on downtown corners or in front of employment offices and telling the passing workers about the failures of American capitalism. The tactic was frequently successful, and the I.W.W. watched its membership grow. Its successes, unsurprisingly, led to its being viewed as a threat by big businesses and their allies in public office. In 1909 and 1910 local governments in Spokane, Washington, and Fresno, California, seeking to end the proselytizing, closed the streets to Wobblies. After well-publicized "free speech fights" in those cities, during which Wobblies were jailed but kept turning out for more street speeches, the two localities gave in.

The San Diego, California, city council nonetheless decided in December 1911 to close a downtown area that had been used for street meetings by the Wobblies and a wide variety of other speakers. The I.W.W. and other groups, including Socialists, single-taxers, and the local branch of the American Federation of Labor, promptly created a Free Speech League. Its purpose was to keep speech alive on the formally closed streets. Some 2,500 people paraded in San Diego in protest on the day the regulation took effect, and Wobblies began flouting the law by speaking in the forbidden zone. The Wobblies gradually assumed leadership of the struggle, for which they were attacked with fire hoses and arrested and brutally beaten, sometimes until they lost consciousness. The police killed one I.W.W. speaker; a local mob tarred another. At one point a mob of armed vigilantes rounded up everyone they suspected of Wobbly affiliation, marched them to a suburb, forced them to kiss the American flag and sing the "Star Spangled Banner," and made them run a gauntlet of clubs and whips. Whitney was outraged. Others were not: the *San Diego Tribune* suggested that all the demonstrators, whom it called "excrement," should be killed.

The Wobblies were victims of state-supported violence, but they were scarcely angelic themselves. Their free speech fights seemed to be designed less to protect speech than to taunt authorities into filling the jails with Wobblies, so that they could be seen as martyrs and gain the resultant publicity. As Anita Whitney's trial would document, individual Wobblies frequently took the law into their own hands. During the San Diego free speech fight some slashed automobile tires and turned downtown San Diego into such an unpleasant place that merchants complained that their customers were avoiding the area. Wobbly rhetoric during the fight was frightening to many in the city and elsewhere. "We are opposed to the existing order; we are against it from bottom up," a Wobbly speaker proclaimed to members of San Diego's First Baptist Church as the violence raged. "We do not respect the laws or flag of the United States. It is a symbol of oppression. . . . We propose to overthrow the whole system and give every man a chance. We do not believe in a God. The preaching of the gospel of Jesus Christ has been the greatest curse in the world because it preaches submission to the present order."

The violence became so bad that California governor Hiram Johnson called for a report by a special investigator. It corroborated all the claims of mistreatment that the Wobblies had made, concluding that their protest had consisted of peaceful if noxious speech but that it had been met with "excessive brutality." San Diego officials countered by asking for help from the U.S. Department of Justice, charging that the Wobblies were conspiring to overthrow the government. The department investigated but, in spite of President William Howard Taft weighing in and declaring that "we ought to take decided action" against the Wobblies, found no evidence of a conspiracy. The fight gradually petered out, but the free speech fights made the Wobblies front-page news throughout the West and elsewhere in the nation. The publicity was not positive; the I.W.W. was increasingly coming to be seen as a threat to civilized society.

To Whitney, the opposition to the free speech fight was a denial of Thomas Jefferson's belief in the importance of speech. "Free speech is free speech," she wrote in the *San Francisco Daily News* in 1926, referring back to those fights. "You either stand for it or you do not. I took it seriously." She took equally seriously the words of I.W.W. and Socialist leaders who went to San Diego to help. The fight made her realize that "the only struggle worthwhile" if men and women were to be free was "the industrial struggle," which would give people "the independence to choose their path in life, and to control the conditions under which they work and live, and . . . this required owning the tools of production." But she did not yet know "how it was to come about."

Californians' perception of threat from the left was exacerbated when, in the spring of 1911, the *Los Angeles Times* building was dynamited. Los Angeles trade unions were engaged in a general strike, aimed at enforcing a closed shop—a system requiring workers in a company to join the workplace union—and the *Times* had been leading a citywide fight against the effort. Twenty-one people were killed in the blast. The police investigation resulted in the arrest of three members of the Structural Iron Workers and Typographical Union and the highly publicized trial of two of them. The I.W.W. called for a general strike to demand their release and blasted the legal system for anti-worker bias. Attorney Clarence Darrow, famed for his courtroom advocacy, was brought in by the unions and got the men to plead guilty in order to avoid the death penalty, although it was unclear whether or not they were actually guilty.

The earlier antiunion feeling in California was strengthened by Californians horrified at the event. A journalist would comment a century later in the *Los Angeles Times* that "in its day, the Times bombing was equivalent to the 2001 destruction of the World Trade Center." Although the police found no evidence of I.W.W. involvement, it was viewed as the most radical of the groups, and its press became particularly bad. "Probably no organization in America was so feared and hated . . . as the I.W.W. before and during the first World War," labor historian Philip Foner noted—or, in Melvyn Dubofsky's words, "The hobo Wobbly had replaced the bearded, bomb-carrying anarchist as a bogeyman in the middle-class American's fevered imagination." Karl Marx and Friedrich Engels had proclaimed in the preamble to *The Communist Manifesto*, a work that the Wobbly leadership knew well, that "A spectre is haunting Europe—the spectre of Communism." That might have been paraphrased in the early decades of the twentieth century as "A specter is haunting the American West—the specter of the Wobblies."

Anita Whitney saw it differently. She supported the I.W.W. because her view was closer to the one reflected in an *Atlantic Monthly* article of 1917: "The American I.W.W. is a neglected and lonely hobo worker, usually malnourished and in need of medical care." To Whitney, the I.W.W.

was a symptom of an industrial society that had run amok, rejecting the humanitarian values she considered to be the underpinnings of the country for which her ancestors had fought. The urban slums she had worked in, the factory conditions she heard and read about: all put her into direct disagreement with the more sanguine view of industrialization held by the majority of Americans in general and of Californians in particular. Whitney was becoming more and more sympathetic to the Wobblies at precisely the moment when popular feeling was turning in the opposite direction. That would be crucial when, only a few years later, she was put on trial.

Her view and the popular image of the I.W.W. came into sharp conflict during the August 1913 Wheatland Hops Riot. The riot took place north of Sacramento, on the Wheatland Ranch run by George Durst, the state's largest agricultural employer. Needing 1,500 workers for the summer harvest, Durst had deliberately advertised for 2,800 and promised high wages. Once 2,800 migrant workers of thirty nationalities appeared, Durst lowered the promised wages to 75 cents a day and occasionally, as the season went on, even less. Two to three hundred of the workers were children. Most of them and their families slept in the open fields, although a few workers were able to rent a tent from Durst for $2.75 a week. The temperature soared to 110 degrees, and there was no water available in the fields. Instead, a Durst cousin sold lemonade for five cents a glass. There were eight fetid outdoor toilets for 2,800 people. Typhoid, dysentery, and diarrhea ran rampant.

There was a nucleus of thirty Wobblies among the workers, and they began a successful drive to organize the others. At the beginning of August a committee was elected to ask Durst for improvements such as better wages, drinking water to be given to the workers in the fields twice a day, and separate toilets for men and women. Durst refused and fired the committee's leaders. A day later, the Wobblies called a camp meeting that drew 2,000 people. While it was still in progress, a frightened Durst, not knowing what would happen next, sent for help. The Yuba County sheriff arrived with a posse that included the local district attorney, who was also Durst's lawyer. Instead of a mob, they found workers and their families singing Wobbly songs. The men nonetheless began elbowing their way through the workers so as to arrest Richard Ford, the chief Wobbly organizer, but had a hard time moving through the angry crowd.

One worried deputy fired a shot in the air, setting off a riot. It resulted in the death of two workers, a deputy, and the district attorney, and in scores of wounded.

The governor responded by sending the National Guard to patrol the ranch for the remainder of the season. Vigilantes raced across California farmlands, terrorizing anyone suspected of sympathizing with the Wobblies, while sheriff's deputies arrested dozens of others all over the state. California newspapers depicted the Wobblies as saboteurs and murderers. Two Wobblies, including one who was not at the meeting, were later convicted of second degree murder and sentenced to life imprisonment. The authorities acknowledged that the men were not physically responsible for the deaths but claimed they had caused the deaths by organizing and using violent language.

A horrified Whitney threw herself into the fight for the men's release, speaking at public meetings and raising money for the I.W.W. defense committee. She joined groups of labor leaders and liberals who pled unsuccessfully with the governor for a pardon. Then, feeling that none of that made any difference to a political and economic system that was hopelessly flawed, Whitney joined the Socialist Party.

Speech in the Streets and at the Supreme Court

When Anita Whitney joined the Socialist Party of America early in 1914, she became one of 118,000 Americans, out of a national population of roughly 100,000,000, who were members that year. There were more and less radical members, but the party itself had a program of collective ownership of transportation, communication, and banking; government ownership of grain elevators and stockyards; legalization of labor unions; fair wages and hours regulations; and participation by the party in the political process.

Relatively small in numbers, the party, formed in 1901, enjoyed an influence larger than its membership would imply. During the first two decades of the twentieth century it was home to a heterogeneous group of anticapitalists that included a large number of Progressive and left-wing labor leaders, African American activists, journalists, and suffragists. At various times, civil rights leaders A. Philip Randolph and Bayard Rustin, labor leaders Sidney Hillman and Walter Reuther, social workers Florence Kelley and Helen Keller, authors Upton Sinclair and Max Eastman, and women's rights activist Inez Milholland all belonged. An estimated 500,000 Americans read the party's weekly *Appeal to Reason*. Two years before Whitney joined, Eugene Debs, the party's frequent candidate for the United States presidency, received 901,551 votes, or 5.97 percent of all those cast. In 1911 the Socialists had campaigned successfully to run the government in thirty-three cities and towns, including Milwaukee, Wisconsin; Butte, Montana; and Flint and Jackson, both in Michigan. By the time Whitney became a Socialist, the party was the third largest in the nation and had elected two members of the U.S. House of Representatives, more than a hundred mayors, and dozens of state legislators.

The party was particularly strong in California and other western states. In 1911 it was running the government in Berkeley and had come close to taking over the city hall of Los Angeles. Debs garnered over 10 percent of the California vote in the 1912 presidential election. When Whitney joined the party there were 8,200 other members in California, in some 300 locals spread throughout the state.

The list of luminaries who were party members and the party's successes at the polls indicated that while socialism was anathema to many Americans, a significantly influential minority thought otherwise. Whitney nonetheless understood that in becoming a socialist, she had left mainstream America behind. It was a decision that had evolved over time and that seemed to her to be the logical culmination of her experiences and her thinking. "Imperceptibly and unconsciously I passed over the line," she later told a colleague who was writing Whitney's biography, "the invisible line, which divides mankind into two different groups, the group which stands for human exploitation and the group which stands for the fullness of life here and now, for human welfare." She decided "to do everything that can be done by constitutional means to change the system." It was her way of remaining true to what she viewed as the ideals of the nation her ancestors had helped to found. She would work within the system in the hope of changing it for the better.

Whitney's membership in the Socialist Party nonetheless appears to have resulted in far less than she had expected. She went to some meetings and distributed some campaign literature, but "I can never remember that we had any real work to do," she remarked to her biographer. "Being a Socialist didn't amount to much in those days." The party was split into pro- and antiwar factions when the United States entered World War I in 1917 in spite of the Socialists' formal opposition to the war, and her antiwar activities took place primarily through other organizations. She was a member of the American Union Against Militarism (AUAM) and treasurer of the San Francisco branch of the People's Council of America for Democracy and Peace, both of which held public antiwar meetings and distributed antiwar literature. She also served as vice president of the Woman's Peace Party of California, the state branch of a national organization headed by Jane Addams. An Oakland police officer would later acknowledge that Whitney was under police surveillance during World War I because of her "pacifist attitude."

Socialism dovetailed nicely with Whitney's support for the Wobblies. Socialists like Debs had been crucial to the founding of the I.W.W. and remained influential in its ranks. Both groups called for the end of what they viewed as an exploitative industrial capitalism and the establishment of a worker-run society. Unlike the Wobblies, however, the Socialists believed in engaging in politics, as the name Socialist Party and its successes in winning elections made clear. The Wobblies, well aware that migratory workers, African Americans in the South, child laborers, and immigrants all lacked voting rights, saw no point to the political process. On that issue Whitney sided with the Socialists. She would maintain a commitment to change through the political process for the rest of her life, although she also believed in direct action such as strikes and demonstrations. In spite of Whitney's and the party's commitment to peaceful change, however, most Californians viewed the party as a violent menace. That perception would affect her trial.

The year 1917 brought another development that delighted Whitney but would also contribute to her being labeled a criminal. When the Russian Bolsheviks seized power in November 1917 and created the Soviet Union, Whitney was enthusiastic. She was excited by the fact that the Bolsheviks were not timid reformers, which was the way she had come to view the American Socialists: in contrast, the Bolsheviks *acted* on socialist principles. Much later, in the 1940s, she would tell her biographer wryly, "Sometimes I wonder how I could have been so enthusiastic—I knew so little." But in 1917 and for some years to come she was a great fan of Russian communism, not as a direct model for the United States but as an indication that the masses all over the world were ready for a more egalitarian society.

Other California Socialist Party members were equally enthusiastic. Under the leadership of state secretary John C. Taylor, who would be called to testify at Whitney's trial, the party's state headquarters had moved in 1916 across San Francisco Bay to Whitney's hometown of Oakland. Taylor's platform, when he ran unsuccessfully for mayor of Oakland in 1919, called for a six-hour workday, establishment of industrial unions, and a socialist city administration backed by a workers', soldiers', and sailors' council. Oakland socialists promised that, if elected, they would take over idle land and industrial plants to provide work for the unemployed. The Alameda county party convention, which drew up the platform, demanded release of political prisoners, withdrawal of American troops from Russia, and unionization of workers on an industrial basis.

Whitney watched the developments in the Soviet Union and supported the California Socialist Party while maintaining a busy schedule of activities at home, all centered around what later generations would call human rights. She was invited to join the executive committee of the Bay Area branch of the National Association for the Advancement of Colored People shortly after the organization was founded in 1909, for example, and remained active in it for fifteen years. To her, opponents of racial equality like the Ku Klux Klan had much in common with the California legislators who had fought against suffrage and jury service for women and who had "forgotten all about the Declaration of Independence" and didn't even know "where to find the bill of rights." They, she thought, were as inept and as far out of touch "as Rip Van Winkle would be in charge of the traffic problem of one of our cities." In 1919 she also accepted the chairmanship of the newly formed American Irish Educational League, a group dedicated to helping Ireland achieve self-determination. She continued as president of the Civic League, served as vice president of the Public Welfare League, and allied herself with the self-styled Left Wing within the Socialist Party.

There had always been a small faction within the Socialist Party that supported revolution rather than evolution. It was energized by the example of the Russian Communists, and in February 1919 the Left Wing issued a manifesto calling for an immediate proletarian revolution— meaning mass strikes. One of the people responsible for the manifesto was Benjamin Gitlow, who would later find himself before the U.S. Supreme Court in a case that would be linked to Whitney's.

As a result of the manifesto, the party fractured into such a complicated conglomeration of factions that the National Executive Committee called an Emergency Convention to be held in Chicago in August. When the convention began, members of the more radical wing made an attempt to take it over. They failed, and many of them were shut out of the meeting. That prompted them to hold their own convention in an I.W.W. hall where, singing the "Internationale" (the international social-

{ *Chapter Two* }

ist anthem) and raising cheers for Debs and for the I.W.W., they formed the Communist Labor Party. Membership in the new party would be open to anyone who paid dues of fifty cents a month, although those unable to pay could ask for a subsidy. Prospective members were also required to sign a pledge both foreswearing membership in any other political party and recognizing "the necessity of the working class organizing itself politically and industrially for the establishment of Communism."

The program adopted at the Communist Labor Party convention supported participation in the political process as a useful propaganda mechanism even as it denigrated the ability of the process to end "the capitalist system" and called for "the establishment of the Dictatorship of the Proletariat." It emphasized "the actions of the masses" in "shops and factories"—translated, that meant strikes—and declared that "the use of the political machinery of the capitalist state" for the purpose of creating the dictatorship of the proletariat was "secondary." The program also endorsed the I.W.W., a decision that would have reverberations when Anita Whitney was brought to trial. In addition, the program pledged allegiance to the Communist International, the international communist organization recently created in Moscow. At the same time, it emphasized that theirs would be a thoroughly American movement, meaning it would focus on political and labor action rather than armed revolution. It rejected violence, sabotage, or terrorism, calling instead for "direct action" that involved workers uniting to force concessions from employers.

The six-man California delegation to the August Socialist Party convention was among those who left its meeting and participated in the organization of the Communist Labor Party. Returning to California, delegation members went around the state urging locals of the Socialist Party to follow their example. In mid-October, the Oakland Socialist Party local of which Whitney was a member voted to leave the party and join what was seen as the more energetic, more ideologically relevant, and more likely to succeed Communist Labor Party instead. The San Francisco local of the new party then called for the formation of a state Communist Labor Party. A founding convention was held in Loring Hall, in what had been the Oakland Socialist Party headquarters, on November 9, 1919, with what Whitney estimated were 150 delegates attending. It was called to order by state secretary John C. Taylor and promptly constituted itself as the California Communist Labor Party (CLP).

The convention was held in a room in Loring Hall that seemed an incongruous choice as the venue for a revolution, which is what California would claim was its purpose. The room did indeed have framed pictures of Karl Marx, Eugene Debs, and other left-wing luminaries on its walls. As the room was sometimes used for social events, though, red crepe paper streamers were strung between the corners of the room and the red globe chandeliers, giving it something of a party air. A piano stood near an old bookcase with glass doors. A silk American flag was hung inside one of the doors, and that too would become important when Anita Whitney was put on trial. According to the *Oakland Enquirer* reporter who covered the convention and bought a copy of the *Communist Manifesto* there, other bookcases in the hall outside the room held copies of the *Manifesto* along with various socialist and I.W.W. publications and a pamphlet by Margaret Sanger on birth control.

Whitney was at the convention as part of the Oakland delegation and as a member of both the credentials and the resolutions committees. One of the proposals that she brought to the floor on behalf of herself and the other resolutions committee members called for the California CLP to emphasize greater participation in the political process, as capturing the machinery of government "can be of tremendous assistance to the workers in their struggle for emancipation; being fully convinced of the utter futility of obtaining any real measure of justice or freedom under officials elected by parties owned and controlled by the capitalist class." It was voted down. Instead, the convention adopted a resolution much like that of the national convention, criticizing political participation as relatively worthless and advocating workers' organizing as the key weapon in the class struggle. Whitney remained at the convention and was elected as an alternate representative to the new party's executive committee.

The proceedings at the convention were thoroughly examined during Whitney's trial and will be discussed later on. For the moment, though, it is important to understand something of the atmosphere in the country generally and in California specifically at the time the convention and the trial took place.

World War I officially ended on November 11, 1918, and the nation as a whole was ready to return to a peaceful and prosperous existence. Instead, it faced a series of events that made many Americans wonder how safe the country really was and led them to endorse what has come to be called the Red Scare of 1919–1920.

While many workers were no doubt as discontented with their lives during the war as they had been before, the AFL adopted a no-strike pledge, and the war years for the most part saw labor restraining itself in the name of the war effort. Now in late 1918, however, the war was over, and organized labor was ready to return to reaping what it saw as its fair share of the national wealth it played such a large part in creating.

In January 1919, 35,000 Seattle shipyard workers went out on strike. Management refused to negotiate about the workers' demand for better wages, and in response the Seattle Central Labor Council called a general strike that paralyzed the city for months. In April, a bomb was sent to the Seattle mayor's house, and another went to the home of a former U.S. senator in Georgia. Thirty-four more bombs addressed to major U.S. officeholders were found in the New York postal system. Fear seized the country. On May 1, when labor is traditionally celebrated across much of the world, May Day protestors in cities across the nation clashed with mobs of citizens and with police. Two protestors were killed in Cleveland, and more than a hundred others were wounded. The following month bombs went off in eight cities. One of them damaged the home of Attorney General A. Mitchell Palmer in Washington, D.C.; another exploded across the street at the residence of then Assistant Secretary of the Navy Franklin Delano Roosevelt. Attorney General Palmer and major American newspapers warned that Bolsheviks were about to take over the country. As historian Samuel Walker has commented, "Summer 1919 was one of the grimmest and most conflict-ridden periods in American history."

As the year continued, so did labor unrest. Police in Boston went out on strike in September when the city refused to let their union affiliate with the AFL. A day of looting and rioting followed. Massachusetts governor Calvin Coolidge sent state police to try to end the strike, which the police decided to call off themselves two days later. U.S. senator Henry Cabot Lodge of Massachusetts nonetheless described the police's action as the first step in turning the country into a Soviet state. "Bolshevism in the United States is no longer a specter. Boston in chaos reveals its sinister substance," the *Philadelphia Public-Ledger* weighed in.

That same month, steelworkers struck, shutting down mills across the country. In October some 400,000 mine workers went out after they and mine owners failed to agree on a contract. President Woodrow Wilson declared the miners' strike "not only unjustifiable but unlawful" and Attorney General Palmer obtained a court injunction ordering the miners back to work. They refused to honor it. Federal troops moved into the mine fields. Eventually, President Wilson imposed a wage increase of 14 percent and established an arbitration commission to deal with other demands, and the workers reluctantly returned to the mines.

The reaction of the country to the strikes was perhaps typified by former president William Howard Taft. Declaring that he supported unionism, Taft nonetheless interpreted the labor unrest as proving that Bolshevism "has penetrated to this country. Because of the presence of hordes of ignorant European foreigners . . . with little or no knowledge of our language, with no appreciation of American civilization . . . it has taken strong hold in many of our congested centres and is the backing of a good many of the strikes from which our whole community is suffering today . . . there are radical men among the labor men who work a great deal more with their mouths than they do with their hands and who are seeking . . . to upset society and to introduce extreme Socialism, anarchy, and Bolshevism into the community." Taft's views no doubt dovetailed with those of a large segment of the American public. Many citizens were convinced that a workers' revolution was imminent and that a foreign ideology, brought to the country's shores by hordes of unwashed immigrants, was about to destroy the nation that had so recently emerged from war.

That conviction was encouraged by Attorney General Palmer, who established a Department of Justice General Intelligence Division to investigate radical activities and put it under the leadership of a young J. Edgar Hoover. Palmer and Hoover's Justice Department would soon round up both citizens and aliens accused of radicalism and deport as many of them as the laws allowed. In the process, the General Intelligence Division exacerbated the country's fear of supposedly Bolshevik-inspired labor activities and "subversive" speech.

Boston attorney Louis Dembitz Brandeis saw the situation differently. The refusal of the giant companies spawned by the industrial revolution to recognize the legitimate demands of workers was the reason for all the unrest, he declared. "Are not these huge trusts large contributing causes to . . . unintelligent expressions of social unrest?" he had written to a correspondent in 1911, expressing a view of the trusts that would last throughout his life. "Is it not irony to speak of the equality of opportunity in a country cursed with their bigness?" To Palmer and Hoover, however, the culprit was the articulation of noxious ideas.

Speech rights had been under assault since the United States Congress declared war on Germany on April 6, 1917. The Selective Service Act of May 1917 required registration of all able-bodied men aged 21–30, and was changed in 1918 to apply to ages 18–45. Anyone who was openly opposed to American involvement in the war or to the draft immediately became suspect. Nonetheless, antiwar voices came from all over the nation. In the South, Populist politician Tom Watson, later a U.S. senator, spoke out against American involvement; so did Robert La Follette, the Progressive U.S. senator from Wisconsin. German Americans with emotional ties to their original homeland, Irish Americans who were opposed to any alliance with Great Britain, Russian immigrants who had left Russia to avoid being conscripted into the czar's army, the American Union Against Militarism, the No Conscription League, the American Socialist Party—all took a strong antiwar, antidraft stance. There were widespread antiwar protests across the country.

Mainstream religious leaders chimed in as well. They were unhappy with the limits of one of the draft law's few exemptions, which applied to members of "any well-recognized religious sect or organization at present organized and existing and whose existing creed or principles forbid its members to participate in war in any form." Such conscientious objectors could be required to perform "noncombatant service," which included working in supply depots, "sanitary detachments," or road-building groups serving combatant units at the front. The religious leaders charged that since the law denied exemptions to conscientious objectors who refused to support the war effort by performing such service, it violated religious liberty. They were joined by pacifists such as

Roger Baldwin, a civil libertarian whose path would soon cross that of Anita Whitney.

The government responded fiercely to the protests. The "authority to exercise censorship is absolutely necessary to the public safety," President Woodrow Wilson proclaimed, and Congress soon enacted the Espionage Act of June 15, 1917. An amalgam of seventeen bills prepared in the attorney general's office, the Act was publicized as a measure that was necessary to stop spies and other subversives. It outlawed collection and transmittal of military information to the country's enemies. It also criminalized willful obstruction of "the recruiting or enlistment service of the United States" and made it punishable by fines of up to $10,000 and prison sentences of up to twenty years. "Obstruction" included speech protesting the draft, as was made clear when the Espionage Act was amended and broadened by the Sedition Act of May 16, 1918. It outlawed not only any attempt to cause "insubordination" or refusal to serve in the armed forces but, in addition, "any disloyal, profane, scurrilous, or abusive language about the form of government of the United States, or the Constitution of the United States, or the military or naval forces . . . or the flag . . . or the uniform of the Army or Navy" or language designed to bring any of the above "into contempt, scorn, contumely, or disrepute." That meant it was suddenly illegal to say, for example, that the draft was unwise or unconstitutional, or that the Constitution should not have legalized slavery, or that the design of the flag should be changed, or that the soldiers' uniforms were not warm enough.

It was not illegal just in theory; some of those words led to prosecutions under the Act. There were more than 2,000 such prosecutions between 1917 and 1921, resulting in over 1,000 convictions. Eugene Debs gave a speech opposing the idea of war and, as we will see, was sentenced to ten years in prison. So was Rose Pastor Stokes, a socialist who had written a letter to the *Kansas City Star* saying, "I am for the people, while the government is for the profiteers." (Debs was in prison for two and a half years; Stokes appealed, and the government abandoned prosecution of her in 1921.) Thirteen people in Philadelphia were charged with treason for circulating a pamphlet entitled "Long Live the Constitution of the United States." A Montana rancher was arrested for saying he would flee rather than fight in the war, which he hoped the Germans would win, because the United States was fighting for Wall Street rather than the average citizen. Filmmaker Robert Goldstein produced a movie about the American Revolution that showed the British as an enemy, leading Seneca Indians in a massacre of colonists during a 1778 battle. He was prosecuted under the act and sentenced to ten years in a California penitentiary. Peter Wimmer was sentenced to six months in jail for saying that the war benefited only Wall Street brokers. He was luckier than Stephen Binder, who published a pamphlet saying essentially the same thing. Binder's sentence was two years in prison. They both fared better than D. T. Blodgett, an Iowa man sentenced to twenty years for a leaflet again arguing that the war served only the interests of capitalists and urging voters not to reelect a congressman who had voted for conscription.

Wobblies came under particular suspicion. Back in 1915, President Wilson had told Congress:

I am sorry to say that the gravest threats against our national peace and safety have been uttered within our own borders. There are citizens of the United States, I blush to admit, born under other flags but welcomed under our generous naturalization laws . . . who have poured the poison of disloyalty into the very arteries of our national life; who have sought to bring the authority and good name of our Government into contempt, to destroy our industries wherever they thought it effective for their vindictive purposes to strike at them, and to debase our politics to the uses of foreign intrigue.

The "destroy our industries" phrase was a clear reference to the I.W.W. It equated Wobblies with immigrants, and the suspicion of radical unionists and "foreigners," whether citizens or not, would be joined in the American mind. Wilson had gone on to urge Congress to enact a law that would enable the government to deal with such disloyalty, and the Espionage and Sedition Acts were the direct result. One section of the Sedition Act, clearly aimed at the Wobblies and other radical unionists, made it illegal to advocate "any curtailment of production in this country of any thing or things, product or products, necessary or essential to the prosecution of the war." It was therefore unsurprising that federal officials used the authority of the Espionage Act to raid I.W.W. headquarters and local halls across the country, claiming that the union's activities were being financed by Germany. They seized records and arrested leaders, ninety-six of whom were convicted of Espionage Act violations on the basis of questionable evidence.

In October 1917, Congress had passed the Trading with the Enemy Act. One of its sections empowered the government to censor any foreign-language publications that contained articles concerning the United States or any nation involved in the war. The post office was given the authority to close the mails to such a publication, unless a full translation of the material was given to and approved by the local postmaster. That effectively reduced the foreign-language press to reporting only pleasantries. Now in 1918 the Sedition Act gave the Postmaster General the power to deny use of the postal system to *any* letters and publications he deemed to be in violation of the Act's prohibitions. The U.S. Postal Service promptly closed the mails to virtually every left-wing, antiwar, and Socialist publication printed. Postmaster General Albert S. Burleson ordered newspapers to be excluded from the mails if they said "that this Government is the tool of Wall Street, or of the munitions makers, or of anybody."

State and local officials soon followed the example of the federal government with regulations, laws, and prosecutions of their own. The Los Angeles Board of Education prohibited the city's schools from allowing any discussion of peace. South Dakota tried and convicted a farmer who had counseled against enlisting in the army because he believed the war to be a Wall Street plot. An Ohio farmer who said that soldiers in American camps were "dying off like flies" was similarly prosecuted. So was a Minnesota man who told women knitting socks for soldiers that "no soldier ever sees these socks," as were Iowa and South Dakota citizens who expressed opposition to the war. Wobblies were routinely jailed by both federal and state officials, particularly those in western states. The language used by legislators seeking or enacting state sedition laws indicates that they equated antiwar activists with Wobblies. The legislator behind the Nebraska law criminalizing disloyal acts or speech said it was "intended to catch the I.W.W. tramps and pool hall habitués." A U.S. congressman from California introduced a bill that, declaring the entire United States to be a war zone, would have made antiwar speech an offense to be tried by court martial and punishable by death. "Hope to Reach I.W.W.," the *New York Times* reported about it.

As historian Paul Murphy has noted, "The story of civil liberties during World War I is a dreary, disturbing, and, in some respects, shocking chapter out of the nation's past," one in which Americans "saw liberty and justice prostituted in ways more extreme and extensive than at any other time in American history." Whitney agreed that it was shocking, and it directly affected her behavior. "It was at this time," she wrote later, "that I acquired the habit of going bail" for Wobblies and others arrested "without rhyme and reason." She decided to "do all in my power to stand for those elemental liberties of which Americans had so fondly and so often boasted—that a man was innocent until proven guilty, and the right of the accused to bail pending his trial."

To California economic and political leaders, the labor activism and left-wing rhetoric were all of a piece, and it was one that they found immensely threatening. Back in 1912, when the report exonerating the I.W.W. from the violence that had taken place during the San Diego speech fights was published, its author had nonetheless called for legislation to stop the Wobblies. The I.W.W., Commissioner Harris Weinstock wrote in the report, used "unholy and reckless methods to attain its ends," which were based on an ideology "imported from the continent of Europe" and which might well "seriously . . . menace the industrial peace and welfare of the country." It was unthinkable to Weinstock, and to many other Americans, that unrest arose from working conditions and economic inequality rather than foreign ideologies. Nonetheless, no immediate legislation resulted.

The Wobblies, however, were less likely than more moderate unionists to forgo protest during the war. There were a number of strikes in western states during 1917 and 1918, and the I.W.W. was blamed for most of them. During those years Wobblies were investigated by both local and federal officials and frequently rounded up. On December 17, 1917, the back porch of the California governor's residence in Sacramento was bombed. Fortunately, there were no injuries, but police arrested all the Wobblies they could find in Sacramento and charged fifty-three of them with the crime. Many were convicted, in spite of the FBI's belief that they were not guilty. Early in 1918 the federal Department of Justice declared that it had uncovered an I.W.W. plot to destroy industries and shipping on the West Coast. The California gubernatorial campaign later that year featured calls by all the candidates for anti-I.W.W. legislation. When William D. Stephens, the winner, was sworn into office on January 7, 1919, he took pains to castigate the Wobblies in his inaugural address. Using a term for the German enemy that had been widely heard during the recent war, Stephens labeled the Wobblies the "Huns of industry" as well as "terrorists," and "skulking wielders of the torch of contemptible setters of time explosions."

His prose may have been somewhat purple but it accurately reflected popular feeling, as witnessed by his election and by what followed next. California newspapers kept up a drumbeat of anti-Wobbly headlines. On January 24, 1919, at the request of the Stephens administration, California senator William Kehoe introduced a criminal syndicalism bill. "Syndicalism," the term used to describe the labor movement's emphasis on strikes and other "industrial" action rather than on working through the political system, was reinterpreted by California (and the seven other states that had already enacted similar legislation) so as to outlaw ideas and speech. The bill defined "criminal syndicalism" as "any doctrine or precept advocating, teaching or aiding and abetting the commission of crime, sabotage (which word is hereby defined as meaning wilful and malicious physical damage or injury to physical property), or unlawful acts of force and violence or unlawful methods of terrorism as a means of accomplishing a change in industrial ownership or control, or affecting any political change." The bill criminalized any spoken, written, or printed words as well as any "personal conduct" that "advocates, teaches or aids and abets criminal syndicalism," along with any involvement in organizing or becoming a member of an organization that did so. It would therefore become illegal in California to *advocate* strikes or industrial sabotage, or to form an organization to discuss such possibilities. The Wobbly songs quoted earlier had suddenly become illegal as well. The punishment for committing such a felony was "not less than one nor more than fourteen years" in the state prison.

A few legislators objected that the bill outlawed advocacy unconnected to any actual illegal acts and would chill legitimate speech. They said as well that it was worded ambiguously and could be used to prosecute legitimate unions. Their objections gained little traction. That was not surprising, given events taking place outside the legislative halls. While the bill was being considered, the I.W.W. was conducting strikes throughout the citrus groves of Southern California, where growers united to drive out "Russian Bolshevik" Wobblies. A report that the I.W.W. was plotting trouble in Los Angeles led the mayor to convene an emergency meeting of police, U.S. Army representatives, and businessmen. Newspapers were giving front-page coverage to the Seattle general strike mentioned earlier. In March, a bomb killed the wife of an Oakland banker who had been threatened in a note that a U.S. marshal said was the work of the Wobblies. The Oakland captain of inspectors declared that the murder—later discovered to be the work of a mentally ill ship worker—was the beginning of a reign of terror by the I.W.W. While the syndicalism bill was couched in general terms, Senator Kehoe, who introduced it, announced that it was intended primarily to "stop the propaganda of an organization known as the Industrial Workers of the World, which seeks to accomplish its objects by acts of terrorism."

It was in that climate that the California criminal syndicalism bill sailed through the legislature with an Assembly vote of 59–9 and a Senate vote of 33–0. It was signed by the governor on April 30, 1919, and went into immediate effect. Seventeen other states also reacted to the hysteria, and helped contribute to it, by passing similar anti-syndicalism laws that year. Fear of the Wobblies, and of their attack on unbounded capitalism, clearly was behind the California law, and was made all the more apparent by the heavy lobbying for it by groups such as the San Francisco Chamber of Commerce, the Los Angeles Chamber of Commerce, the Los Angeles Better American Federation, and the Merchants and Manufacturers' Association.

Within ten days, Wobblies in San Francisco and Oakland were being charged under the new statute. The Alameda County district attorney quickly obtained warrants for forty Oakland men. One of them was John Taylor, the CLP secretary described in the *San Francisco Chronicle* as an "alleged I.W.W. agitator." Warrants in hand, Oakland police captain Walter J. Peterson told the press that he expected to have the city "cleaned of I.W.W.s" within a few hours.

Other "alleged agitators" were seized without warrants. "Militant working men and men suspected of radical leanings were arrested without warrants and lodged in jail," Whitney recalled. "The organizers of the Socialist Party were arrested without warrants in the middle of the night." Whitney used her "small resources" to post bail for them, over and over again. Then, in November 1919, Anita Whitney found herself in jail.

Anyone reading about people tried for exercising their speech rights might wonder, from the vantage point of the twenty-first century, why judges allowed any of those people to go to prison. After all, the First Amendment to the Constitution, which says that "Congress shall pass no law . . . abridging the freedom of speech, or of the press, or the right of the people peaceably to assemble, and to petition the Government for a redress of grievances" had been in existence since 1791. That would seem to mean that the Constitution limits the ability of the national government not only to stifle speech but also to interfere with people gathering to discuss political or other issues and to complain when they find governmental action unacceptable, and yet the Espionage Act clearly abridged both speech and press. The Supreme Court had declared as early as 1803 (*Marbury v. Madison*) that the federal judiciary was the final arbiter of the Constitution. Where was the Court in all of this?

The short answer is that the Supreme Court upheld the constitutionality of the Espionage Act and the convictions under it. The long answer, explaining why it did so, is a bit more complicated.

The American national government was a relatively hands-off one well into the beginning of the twentieth century. Americans at the time of the writing of the Constitution were suspicious of centralized power, which is why they adopted a Constitution of enumerated powers; that is, they gave the federal government only the powers specifically listed in the Constitution. Thinking that might not be enough to keep federal power in check, they went further and ratified a Bill of Rights that spells out strict limitations on the national government. It includes not only the First Amendment's guarantee of speech but, for example, the Fourth Amendment's prohibition of unreasonable searches and seizures and the Eighth Amendment's ban on cruel and unusual punishments. The Tenth Amendment ("The powers not delegated to the United States by the Constitution, nor prohibited by it to the states, are reserved to the states respectively, or to the people") left what constitutional scholars call the "police powers"—powers over health, safety, welfare, education—to the states. The federal government could not abridge the rights to speech or any of the other rights included in the Bill of Rights, but the Constitution said nothing about what the states could do. That meant that any regulation of the rights guaranteed by the Bill of Rights was left to the states, which would have a monopoly over interference with rights such as speech unless they were limited by their own constitutions and statutes. Chief Justice John Marshall gave the formal imprimatur to the states' monopoly when he declared in 1833, in *Barron v. Baltimore*, that the Bill of Rights was binding only on the federal government, not the states. It didn't matter that the First Amendment failed to spell out exactly what was meant by freedom of speech, as only the federal government was prohibited from abridging it. The states, exercising their police powers, could still criminalize speech such as obscenity or libel or anything else they considered inimical to the public welfare.

The national government became more powerful during the late nineteenth and early twentieth centuries, primarily in response to the growth of industrialization that also led to the creation of the I.W.W. The Progressive Era of those years was epitomized by a political ideology that emphasized the duty of the government to alleviate the worst side effects of industrialization and create a just society by, for example, establishing protection for women and child laborers, mandating food and drug safety, and regulating trusts. While much of the efforts of Progressives were geared toward states and localities and included precisely the kinds of issues in which Anita Whitney was involved—better conditions for tenement dwellers, creation of a juvenile justice system, woman suffrage—they also lobbied successfully for legislation at the federal level. While that resulted in an enlarged federal bureaucracy, it also engendered a recognition among many Americans that a more activist central government could be a boon as well as a problem. That, as we will see, would have an effect on Americans' attitudes toward the regulation of speech.

There was one important pre–World War I occasion on which the federal government did regulate speech. In 1798, the young national government passed the Alien and Sedition Acts, under which antigovernment speech and press were curtailed. Interestingly, in light of the passage of the Espionage and Sedition Acts during the First World War, the earlier Alien and Sedition Acts were enacted when it was widely assumed that the United States would soon go to war with France. The earlier Acts also included anti-immigrant provisions that gave the president the power to deport aliens he considered to be dangerous. The constitutionality of the early Sedition Act, which expired in 1801, was never tested in the Supreme Court. It was widely viewed as an unfortunate aberration, and from 1798 to 1917 the federal government rarely moved into the area of speech or other civil liberties. In fact, according to Roger Baldwin, one of the founders of the American Civil Liberties Union, the phrase "civil liberties" was not part of the American vocabulary before World War I. In 1916 Harvard Law School professor Zechariah Chafee, whom we will meet again in chapter 5, surveyed speech cases in the federal courts and discovered there were almost none. The issue of whether or under what circumstances the federal government could prohibit speech simply had not been considered by the Supreme Court.

The Court had, however, made a statement about the constitutional meaning of freedom of speech. Some Americans thought that the Fourteenth Amendment's due process clause ("No state shall . . . deprive any person of life, liberty, or property, without due process of law") meant that states, too, were forbidden to interfere with liberties such as speech unless they could demonstrate a convincing reason for doing so. The Supreme Court rejected that idea in 1907, in a case called *Patterson v. Colorado*. Thomas Patterson had published articles and a cartoon that criticized Colorado Supreme Court judges, claiming among other things that two of them were in their positions illegally. He was convicted of contempt of court. Patterson challenged the conviction under both the state and the federal constitutions, citing the Fourteenth Amendment. Justice Oliver Wendell Holmes Jr., writing for the Court, held that "even if we were to assume that freedom of speech and of the press were protected from abridgments on the part not only of the United States but of the states," a position that Holmes and the Court did not adopt, Patterson had no case. The reason was that the constitutional guarantee of freedom of speech was no more than a limit on prior restraints; that is, the government could not prevent a speaker from speaking. Holmes took the notion of prior restraint as the only limitation on the government's power to control speech directly from the works of eighteenth-century English jurist William Blackstone and subsequent English law. The government could, however, punish the speaker after the fact if it determined that the speech was, in Holmes's words, "deemed contrary to the public welfare." Scholars would come to call that the "bad tendency" test: if the speech tended to—might possibly lead in the future to—something a legislature considered "bad," it could be punished. The only dissenter in the Colorado case was Justice John Marshall Harlan, who argued that "the privileges of free speech and of a free press, belonging to every citizen of the United States, constitute essential parts of every man's liberty. . . . It is, I think, impossible to conceive of liberty, as secured by the Constitution against hostile action, whether by the nation or by the states, which does not embrace the right to enjoy free speech and the right to have a free press." Harlan would have held that the right to free speech was binding on the states. He was in a minority of one, however, and so for the moment, the rule of law was that states could punish speech.

That was the situation in 1919 when the Supreme Court heard *Schenck v. United States*, its first case involving the Espionage Act of 1917. Charles Schenck was the general secretary of the Socialist Party. He was convicted for hindering the war effort by publishing a two-page leaflet calling the draft a violation of the Thirteenth Amendment's prohibition of involuntary servitude. Some of the leaflets were available to anyone who wandered into the party's bookshop on Arch Street in Philadelphia; some 15,000 others were mailed to men who had passed their physicals for the draft. Justice Holmes, writing in 1919 for what this time was a unanimous court, declared that if Schenck had distributed the leaflet in peacetime, his act might have been legal. However, "the character of every act depends upon the circumstances in which it is done," Holmes declared. "When a nation is at war many things that might be said in time of peace are such a hindrance to its effort that their utterance will not be endured so long as men fight and that no Court could regard them as protected by any constitutional right." Then he penned words destined to be famous: "The most stringent protection of free speech would not protect a man in falsely shouting fire in a theatre and causing panic." He continued with what would be known as the clear and present danger test: "The question in every case is whether the words used are used in such circumstances and are of such a nature as to create a clear and present danger that they will bring about the substantive evils that Congress has a right to prevent."

The problem with Holmes's formulation was that he did not define "clear" or "present" or "danger." One of the functions of the Supreme Court is to give guidance to lower courts in interpreting the Constitution and other laws. The vague clear and present danger test provided no such guidance. Supreme Court Justice Robert Jackson, referring to the test three decades later, commented, "All agree that it means something very important, but no two seem to agree on what it is." The doctrine in fact became something of an ideological Rorschach test, allowing people of widely differing opinions to interpret it in ways that reflected their own attitudes toward speech. It was certainly an attitude stemming from something like hysteria about homeland security that led to the prosecution of Schenck and four of his colleagues, many of whose leaflets had been stopped by the postal system and whose action could not be shown to have had any effect on anyone. The "falsely shouting fire in a theatre" example provides no useful guidelines for cases such as Schenck's, where there was no danger of causing a panic that could easily result in people being hurt. Federal authorities, in the person of the postal system, knew about Schenck's pamphlets, and there was adequate time to respond to the opinions in them. Whatever danger Schenck may have presented to the Republic appears to have been substantially less than either clear or present. Holmes, writing that "the document would not have been sent unless it was intended to have some effect," was relying on the bad tendency test. The "clear and present danger" doctrine may have read like a renunciation of the bad tendency test. It was not, at least as applied to Mr. Schenck.

Justice Louis Dembitz Brandeis, whose thinking about speech would be so important to Anita Whitney, was one of the justices who silently concurred in the Schenck case. He went along as well with the Court's next two Espionage Act decisions, in *Frohwerk v. United States* and *Debs v. United States.*

Jacob Frohwerk and a colleague were convicted of violating the Espionage Act by writing and circulating articles, published in the newspaper *Missouri Staats Zeitung* in 1915, that were allegedly designed to cause disloyalty in the armed forces. Like Schenck, Frohwerk questioned the legality of the draft, and he depicted the war as having been caused by a combination of American capitalists and England. He was so certain that his articles were legal, particularly as the ideas for some of them came from speeches reported in the *Congressional Record*, that he sent the newspaper to the Justice Department office in Kansas City each week. Members of Congress quoted in the *Congressional Record* could not be tried for sedition (the Constitution prohibits arresting them for their speech) but ordinary citizens could. It is indicative of the atmosphere in Kansas City that a jury took only three minutes to find Frohwerk guilty. The Supreme Court upheld his conviction and ten-year sentence. Justice Holmes once again wrote for the Court. He admitted that "it does not appear that there was any special effort to reach men who were subject to the draft" and the newspaper was one of "small circulation." Nonetheless, "on that record [of the trial] it is impossible to say that it might not have been found that the circulation of the paper was in quarters where a little breath would be enough to kindle a flame and that the fact was known and relied upon by those who sent the paper out."

Indicating that he stood by his language in the *Schenck* case, Holmes added that "as the language of the article goes there is not much to choose between expressions to be found in them and those before us in Schenck v. United States." In other words, "clear and present danger"— although Holmes did not explicitly use the phrase in *Frohwerk*—meant a person could spend ten years in prison for expressing opinions about the draft that might not have been read by anyone who had been drafted or was eligible for the draft.

The plaintiff in *Debs v. United States* (1919) was of course much better known. Justice Holmes once again wrote for a unanimous court in upholding Eugene Debs's conviction under the Espionage Act for a fiery antiwar speech he had given in Canton, Ohio. The speech had, Holmes said, consisted in large part of "personal experiences and illustrations of the growth of socialism, a glorification of minorities, and a prophecy of the success of the international socialist crusade, with the interjection that 'you need to know that you are fit for something better than slavery and cannon fodder.'" The last phrase and similar language were sufficient proof for Holmes and his colleagues of Debs's intent to obstruct the draft, and Holmes cited *Schenck* and *Frohwerk* in holding that the conviction had to stand. The court was relying once again on the bad tendency test, with Holmes writing that Debs "used words tending to obstruct the recruiting service." At his trial, Debs had declared, "I believe in the right of free speech, in war as well as in peace. . . . I would under no circumstances suppress free speech. It is far more dangerous to attempt to gag the people than to allow them to speak freely what is in their hearts." The Supreme Court clearly disagreed.

As of November 28, 1919, then, when Anita Whitney was arrested under California's criminal syndicalism law, the Supreme Court of the United States had held that the First Amendment prohibitions applied primarily to prior restraints on speech, that states were not subject to the restrictions of the First Amendment, and that opponents of the war could be imprisoned for their speech.

CHAPTER THREE

Anita Whitney Goes to Court

The founding meeting of the California Communist Labor Party took place on November 9, 1919. On November 10, the *Oakland Enquirer* carried a story describing it, written by a seventeen-year-old reporter and university student named Edward Condon. Condon's account quickly became the undisputed source of public knowledge about the event. The article described the meeting as being filled with "Germans and near-Germans" and the program that was adopted as advocating "destruction of private property rights by force." The mental picture conjured up by the description was bad enough for some of the people of Oakland, reading the article only a year after the end of the country's war with Germany. Even worse, however, was what Condon reported next: "The American flag hung in one corner of the room in an antique cabinet and over it was a naval service flag with one star. But during the noon hour, a huge red cloth was hung over the case so that the American flag was no longer visible while the radicals prepared to adopt their un-American constitution."

That did it for some readers. Not only had the Socialists—now the CLP—been running a kitchen in Loring Hall to feed strikers in the Bay area, but they were apparently disrespecting the flag and planning general anarchy as well. The next day, November 11, Americans celebrated their first Armistice Day, commemorating the end of World War I hostilities in western Europe. After midnight, a mob of World War I veterans who had been celebrating at a dance left it to raid Loring Hall. They locked the janitor in a room and proceeded to wreck the hall, smashing open desks and tossing books, pamphlets, and typewriters onto a roaring fire outside. The CLP leaders had been warned about the impending raid and asked repeatedly for police protection, but no officers of the law appeared. Instead, on November 13, commissioner of public health and safety F. F. Morse announced that he was forming a "police loyalty bureau" to root out subversive activities. It would be headed by Detective Fenton Thompson, who would become a key player in the Whitney drama. The city council chimed in on November 15, enacting an ordinance prohibiting meetings in public without a police permit and ordering the police to "exterminate anarchy." Police raided the offices of the CLP and seized its records. Some of Whitney's fellow CLP members were arrested and charged with violating the syndicalism law.

Anita Whitney was a respected figure in Oakland and throughout much of California. Her work on behalf of suffrage and her other community activities were well known, but now so was her membership in the CLP, and that made her a contentious figure. So did her role as treasurer of the Labor Defense League, organized to help in the defense of people—primarily Wobblies—charged under the state criminal syndicalism law. As the Wobblies had done in the free speech fights, the League protested what it saw as an attempt to keep workers from speaking out. "These are the most trying times for all of us interested in the working class movement," a League letter asking for donations read. "Laws are being passed to suppress all of our activities and even our freedom of expression."

Whitney's freedom of expression was in fact about to be curtailed. Invoking the new permit requirement, Police Chief J. F. Lynch prevailed on the Oakland Mothers' Club to cancel a speech Whitney had planned to present about "Women in Legislation." Later in November, the Oakland Center of the California Civic League that she had helped to found was scheduled to hear her lecture at the Hotel Oakland on "The Negro Problem in the United States." Police Chief Lynch tried to get that speech called off as well. The League protested, with its board of directors insisting that its members had a constitutional right to hear Whitney. The board was also concerned about what a decision to bar Whitney might do to her reputation. "The board of Oakland Center feels that it is sitting in the capacity of a jury," Oakland Center president Annie Law said. "As we decide so Miss Whitney will forever be stamped before the community. Unless there is evidence that she has committed disloyal acts we believe we, as women, have no right to brand her . . . we cannot do serious injury to a woman who has done so much for women and girls as has Miss Whitney without authentic information." Some of the members spoke to Whitney, who told them that she was not and never had been a member of the I.W.W. She added, "I love the United States. I love the American flag, I am a loyal American citizen and I want an American flag on the platform upon which I am to stand."

The League finally got an agreement from the police department that the speech could go on as long as a police officer was present and the American flag was displayed. Commissioner Morse, overruling Chief Lynch, nonetheless warned Mrs. Law that Whitney would be held "strictly to account for any unlawful or seditious statements that she may make." "Miss Whitney will not be allowed to say anything unpatriotic or defy constituted authority in any way," Lynch added. A group calling itself the League of Americans, saying it represented members of the American Legion, the Grand Army of the Republic, Veterans of the Foreign Wars, and other veteran groups, then weighed in. It charged that Whitney's position in what the group called the "I.W.W. Labor Defense League" should be sufficient to keep her from speaking. Mrs. Law replied that there was no proof that Whitney was not a loyal American and that the final decision about her appearance would be made on the morning of November 28, the day of the lecture.

Detective Thompson was waiting in the hotel lobby when Whitney arrived that day, as were two deputies and a Department of Justice agent. The detective demanded that Whitney leave without speaking. She refused. Thompson then followed her into the meeting and told the Civic League audience that Whitney had carried food and radical literature to men imprisoned on Alcatraz Island. "Can any of you say that she is not an IWW?" he asked, making it clear that Thompson considered her support for the Wobblies rather than her membership in the CLP to be her real offense. A debate among the audience members ensued, after which the assembled women voted 94 to 48 to hear Whitney speak. The woman who was to have presided, the wife of an Oakland superior court judge, announced that as she was 100 percent American she could not do so. Another League member had to step in for her.

Whitney, undeterred, proceeded to deliver her speech. The meeting had been closed to anyone not a member of the Civic League—others were so eager to get into the room that the shouts and the pounding on the doors by those excluded had at times made it difficult to hear the speakers—but now the doors were thrown open to the public, some of whom may have been drawn as much by the intrigue as by the subject matter. Whitney ignored the drama and gave them a lecture about the plight of "Negroes." Rejecting notions of Negro inferiority, she offered her audience statistics on the underfunding of Negro schools in the South and the lack of economic and political opportunity. She charged that 2,580 men and 50 women had been lynched since 1890, and went on to quote a gripping eyewitness account of a lynching. Pleading for support of a federal antilynching law then being considered by Congress, she said it was necessary "for the fair name of America that this terrible blot on our national escutcheon may be wiped away." "Let us then both work and fight," she concluded, "so that the flag that we love may truly wave 'O'er the land of the free and the home of the brave.'"

The event having ended on that patriotic note, Whitney and a colleague began to leave the hotel. They were stopped by Inspector Thompson and another police officer. "You are under arrest," Thompson told Whitney, on charges of criminal syndicalism. The ostensible reason was her participation in the California Communist Labor Party.

The question of whether to arrest her had been contentious. Thompson had asked Walter Peterson, now serving as the Oakland chief of police, for permission to make the arrest. Peterson refused. He was very much in favor of the criminal syndicalism act but did not see Whitney as a legitimate target. "I investigated Anita Whitney's record," he said later. "I found that she had always done an enormous amount of good in the community. I wasn't in sympathy with her pacifistic ideas and a lot of her other notions. But I recognized that it wasn't in her nature to commit violence nor to encourage it. She was one of those idealists who want to make the world better for everyone." Thompson went over Peterson's head to Commissioner Morse, who was apparently less inclined to see Whitney as well intentioned and told the detective to arrest her.

Now Whitney asked her companion to turn back and get Gail Laughlin, the California Civic League's president, who was also an attorney. The women and the two officers then walked through the cool late afternoon shadows to the police office in City Hall. Whitney was left there while the two other women sought an order setting bail and the cash needed for it. By the time they returned, she had been confined to a cell in the city jail, located on another floor of the building, and it was some hours before they could find someone with the authority to free her.

Whitney knew and trusted Gail Laughlin from the days when they had worked to draft a bill enabling California women to serve as jurors. Laughlin was a general practitioner, however. She was not the right person to represent a defendant in a criminal action, and it was clear that Whitney would now need a defense attorney. Whitney appeared in a crowded courtroom the following morning, accompanied by a group of supporters, and asked police judge George Samuels to put off her arraignment while she searched for a lawyer. The arraignment was rescheduled for four days later, on December 3. As Whitney left the courtroom she told reporters waiting in the corridor, "It has never occurred to me that I could be thought less than a patriotic American citizen."

The photograph of Whitney accompanying the *Oakland Tribune*'s banner headline reporting on the proceedings shows a tall, unsmiling 52-year-old woman with round rimless spectacles perched on her unlined face. Her hair is covered by a large velvet hat and her V-neck coat has velvet lapels. The background indicates that the photo was posed in a photographer's studio. It suggests that the image Whitney chose to present of herself was that of a serious, very respectable citizen.

But the respectable citizen suddenly had to find a criminal defense lawyer in a hurry. Whitney turned to another of her friends, J. E. Pemberton, an elderly gray-haired socialist who had been a country judge. Laughlin and Pemberton represented her in the early stages of the case, reluctantly, fully understanding that neither was equipped to handle a criminal charge. As it turned out, Pemberton was to be more involved in the case than either he or Whitney had hoped.

Whitney was duly arraigned. On December 8 Judge Samuels presided over what the *Los Angeles Times* called a "sensational" preliminary hearing, held to decide whether there was sufficient evidence to justify a trial. Samuels had to struggle to keep the courtroom in order, as well-wishers from the Irish League, the NAACP, and both San Francisco and Oakland chapters of the Civic League jockeyed for the seats that could not accommodate them and all the other eager spectators. The judge had repeatedly to clear the courtroom of standees.

Those who remained inside heard testimony from three reluctant prosecution witnesses, including alleged or admitted members of the Communist Labor Party. The witnesses acknowledged that Whitney was a member of the resolutions and credentials committees at the Loring Hall convention. Journalist Condon testified about the red-covered flag in the bookcase, and Police Inspector William F. Kyle identified various pieces of literature that had been taken from the hall and from Whitney's home after her arrest. Detective Thompson was there and, according to the *Oakland Tribune*, "prompted" the deputy attorney general in charge of presenting the prosecution's case. Whitney's lawyers chose not to mount a defense, and Judge Samuels said he would hand down his decision on December 11 about whether to bind Whitney over for trial.

Oakland was stormy on December 11, but long before the courtroom doors opened at 9 A.M. the corridors were again filled with supporters and curious onlookers. Judge Samuels told the packed courtroom that the CLP, which he labeled "a personal challenge to law and order of the country," was dedicated to revolution and in violation of the syndicalism law. Chastising Whitney, he called her "a person of more than ordinary intelligence" who had to have known exactly what she was doing when she participated in organizing the CLP. Whitney would have to stand trial on five counts under the criminal syndicalism act: organizing and being a member of an organization to advocate, teach, and abet criminal syndicalism; printing matter that advocated, taught, and abetted criminal syndicalism; advocating, teaching, and abetting "unlawful methods of terrorism as a means of accomplishing a change in industrial ownership and control, and as a means of effecting a political change"; justifying criminal syndicalism and such unlawful methods of terrorism; and "by personal acts and conduct" advising, advocating, teaching, and abetting such a change in industrial ownership and the political system.

Judge Samuels set bail at $2,000. Whitney refused to post bail and was taken off to jail, telling reporters, "It is not I but the constitutional rights of all of us that are on trial. Shall we be denied free speech? I believe that is the question, and the paramount one, to be determined."

That may have seemed the paramount question to Whitney, but for the moment the crucial one for Pemberton was how to keep his client out of jail. Two friends of Whitney's did post bail for her, and so she spent only a few hours behind bars, but that was just a temporary solution. Deciding to attack the statute, Pemberton immediately filed an application for a writ of habeas corpus ("produce the body") with

Superior Court Judge James G. Quinn, who was assigned to Whitney's trial and now took over from Judge Samuels. The grounds were not free speech but the alleged invalidity of the law under the California constitution. It specified that only one offense could be mentioned in any criminal statute and, according to Pemberton, the syndicalism law criminalized two different offenses: syndicalism and sabotage. Unfortunately for Pemberton and his client, the California courts had already declared the law to be constitutional.

Trial was set for Tuesday, January 27. During the intervening days, Pemberton searched without initial success for a criminal lawyer and filed motions designed to limit the damage. On January 6 he moved to dismiss the case as improper, because the charges did not contain a "statement of the acts constituting the alleged offense in ordinary or concise language or in such manner as to enable a person of common understanding to know what is intended," and that was in violation of the California Penal Code. In other words, while the indictment incorporated the language of the syndicalism law, it neither mentioned the CLP nor detailed the specific acts of which Whitney was accused. Pemberton filed a motion on January 13 asking for a bill of particulars for each of the counts. The fifth count, for example, charged that Whitney "unlawfully, willfully, wrongfully, deliberately and feloniously by personal acts and conduct" aided criminal syndicalism "with intent to accomplish a change in industrial ownership and control and effecting a political change." Exactly what acts were referred to? The second count accused her of printing, circulating, and displaying books and other printed matter fostering criminal syndicalism. Specifically, what were the publications? On January 16 Whitney submitted an affidavit saying, "I do not advocate, and never have advocated, knowingly the accomplishment of any political change, or any change in industrial ownership or control by means of crime, sabotage, violence, or unlawful methods of terrorism: I have favored, advocated, approved, justified, or attempted to justify no means for any such change or changes other than the use of the ballot and other legal and peaceful means." She also pointed out that the arrest warrant and the evidence presented in police court "refer only to occurrences taking place on the 9th day of November, 1919" but the charges referred to November 28. Without a bill of particulars, therefore, "neither I nor he [Pemberton] can intelligently prepare for trial: and without such information a fair trial cannot be had."

The motions were all denied.

The political atmosphere in California and much of the nation in the months before the trial and during it had only worsened. The California press was particularly strident in its attacks on the I.W.W. and on anyone suspected of being a radical. Calling the Wobblies "America's Cancer Sore," for example, the *Los Angeles Times* printed a cartoon showing a husky uniformed American soldier stomping on a rattlesnake. The cartoon was titled "Stamp the Life Out of It!" The *San Francisco Chronicle* ran front-page headlines like "War to Death on Reds." It too published incendiary cartoons. One, in its December 11 issue, was labeled "Stamp 'Em Out!" and showed large red rats attacking a powerful American leg. The *Oakland Tribune* urged, "Make A Clean Sweep!" and depicted a large broom sweeping dustballs and people labeled "Revolutionary Propaganda," "I.W.W. Assassins," and "Red Murderers" out of the United States. Another of its cartoons showed a smiling Uncle Sam sending 249 "Reds" off to Russia on a Soviet Ark, while he called, "Hurry Back Capt' and Get Another Load." The *San Francisco Chronicle* picked up on the anti-immigrant theme with a cartoon showing Uncle Sam stirring a huge "U.S. Melting Pot," skimming Reds out of the top of it.

While California newspapers were doing their best to lash readers—including, presumably, those who would sit on Whitney's jury—into a frenzy of fear, authorities were rounding up and prosecuting Wobblies. James McHugo, the secretary of the Oakland I.W.W., was one of those put on trial and convicted. On December 7, while Whitney was awaiting trial, McHugo was sentenced to one to fourteen years in San Quentin. The judge in the case was the same James Quinn who would preside over Whitney's trial and, a few months later, over the trial and conviction of John C. Taylor, the CLP secretary who was also called as a witness in Whitney's case. Some of the prosecution witnesses in McHugo's trial would testify in Whitney's, as would Detective Thompson, and Judge Quinn permitted the prosecution to introduce as evidence the kind of "radical" literature that would also feature in the Whitney trial. In sentencing McHugo, Judge Quinn equated criminal syndicalism with treason, declaring, "I believe the criminal syndicalism law is just and that violators of this law commit treasonable crime." The judge did not need to mention that under American law, treason is punishable by death.

Federal authorities, too, were adding to a climate in which Whitney and other CLP and I.W.W. members were unlikely to receive a fair trial. On November 7, 1919, in furtherance of what was mentioned earlier as the Red Scare of 1919–1920, Attorney General Palmer's Department of Justice had raided offices in twelve cities of an organization called the Union of Russian Workers, rounding up hundreds of alleged radicals. That was followed, on January 2, 1920, by the arrest of thousands of suspected subversives in more than forty cities across the nation. Most of those arrested were held incommunicado, without access to their families or any lawyers. The *San Francisco Chronicle* published an article listing more than 500 people who had been arrested and were facing possible deportation. Oakland's loyalty squad was responsible for twenty of the arrests. The arrests themselves and the subsequent treatment of those arrested were so outrageous that a group of twelve leading legal scholars, including Harvard University Law School professors Felix Frankfurter, Roscoe Pound, and Zechariah Chafee Jr. published a book entitled *Report upon the Illegal Practices of the United States Department of Justice*. It documented what it called the Justice Department's "utterly illegal" and unconstitutional acts "which have caused widespread suffering and unrest" and "have struck at the foundation of American free institutions." Attorney General Palmer ignored the critics and orchestrated a propaganda campaign, peaking in late January, that included sending antiradical articles and cartoons to the country's newspapers and magazines; quite possibly some of those in the California press came from that effort.

Across the country, knowing nothing about Whitney's arrest but well aware of the popular panic and the government crackdown, a concerned jurist lamented the events sweeping the nation. Supreme Court Justice Louis D. Brandeis, writing from Washington to his sister-in-law Susan Goldmark on December 7, 1919, compared the Red Scare to the reign of terror led by Spanish Inquisition official Tomas de Torquemada. He lambasted "the intensity of the frenzy . . . of hysterical, unintelligent fear." "It will pass," Brandeis wrote, "but the sense of shame and of sin should endure." Dean Acheson, the justice's law clerk and later secretary of state, asked Brandeis whether police harassment of socialists and trade unionists discouraged his hopes for democracy in the United States. Brandeis denied being discouraged but replied that he was "'simply deeply humiliated and filled with a sense of sin that we with the greatest possibilities of any people should waste ourselves on these age-old methods of oppression.'" Eight years later Brandeis would tell his compatriots exactly why such events were shameful in a democratic society and, in doing so, would become crucial to Anita Whitney's life.

That did not help Whitney in 1920, however, and the atmosphere was tense when her trial began on January 27. There were a few local voices of support for her. The Northern California branch of the NAACP had issued a statement after Whitney was indicted, "declaring its unwavering faith" in Whitney's "true Americanism . . . and her loyalty and devotion to the cause of justice and the common rights of citizenship to all classes." The Women's Irish Educational League of San Francisco had done the same, asserting that

> to persecute an apostle of right and justice who has devoted years of her life to the poor, the lowly and unfortunate is a stain upon real Americanism which should not be tolerated by honest thinking citizens. To permit the stigma of crime to be placed on the character of one of California's best loved and most highly respected women by overambitious police detectives is an outrage that should not be permitted even under the guise of "war-hysteria."

The San Francisco legal council of the Friends of Irish Freedom, certain that Whitney had been singled out in part because of her interest in Irish nationalism, pledged its support for her as well. But those voices were in the minority.

Pemberton was Anita Whitney's sole counsel throughout the pre-trial stage of the case. Gail Laughlin had left it after the preliminary hearing and was busy out of state. Whitney was still unrepresented by anyone with experience in criminal law. Trying a bit desperately to find such a person, Pemberton had asked the court to delay the trial until early April. The request was denied. Just days before the trial began, help came from Fremont Older, the editor of William Randolph Hearst's

San Francisco Call, who had gotten to know Whitney when they were involved in various California social reform campaigns. Older prevailed upon Thomas M. O'Connor to come into the case. Pemberton agreed to remain on the case for a while to aid O'Connor, although, as he would tell the court, he could do no more than participate in a very secondary capacity and expected to leave altogether as soon as O'Connor took over fully.

O'Connor was a charming, stocky man with a thick head of black hair. After boyhood on a farm, he moved to San Francisco at age 19 to read law in a law office and was admitted to the bar in 1891. (In the nineteenth and early twentieth centuries, many would-be lawyers received their legal education by working and studying in a law office rather than going to law school.) He soon began to specialize in criminal law. O'Connor was eloquent enough to have been called "the boy orator of the Mission" by the press and successful enough to have earned the reputation of never having lost a case. He knew what it was to be a prosecutor as well. For some years before 1912, he was a special prosecutor for the State Board of Pharmacy, focusing on prosecuting drug dealers. O'Connor subsequently returned to the defense bar and successfully defended a number of radicals.

The prosecution in the Whitney case also had distinguished lawyers. Ironically enough, the Alameda County district attorney nominally in charge of the prosecution was Ezra Decoto Jr., the man who had replaced Whitney as Alameda County juvenile probation officer when the position became a paid one. He was not actively involved in the case, however, turning it over instead to Deputy Attorney General John U. Calkins and Deputy District Attorney Myron Harris.

Calkins, who occasionally taught law at the University of California–Berkeley, had been an assistant city attorney in Oakland before enlisting in World War I. He was sent to France as a first lieutenant in a machine gun battalion and, in the years following the Whitney trial, published a history of the battalion dedicated to those who had been killed in action. He returned to Oakland early in 1919 and immediately went to work as assistant district attorney of Alameda County, serving on the prosecution team that successfully tried James McHugo before Judge Quinn.

Myron Harris was a native Californian. He had played football and rugby at the University of California, where he attended undergraduate and law school. The son of an Alameda County judge, Harris joined the district attorney's office right after graduating from law school. He soon acquired a reputation for winning most of his cases and would be described by the press as a "'hard-driving' prosecutor." That reputation would only be enhanced by his performance in the Whitney case.

When the Superior Court of the State of California in and for the County of Alameda, Department No. 5, convened on Tuesday, January 27, the strong emotions raised by the case were very much in evidence. The morning air was a bit nippy—only in the high 40s—but a large crowd was at the court even before the doors were opened. Dozens of Whitney supporters, mocked by the press as "fashionably dressed society women," had shown up for all the preliminary hearings, and they were out in force again. On the other side George Price, secretary of the Oakland Post of the American Legion, had sent out a call for ex-servicemen to appear as well. The result was that more than 200 would-be spectators were turned away for lack of seats.

As soon as the proceedings began, Thomas O'Connor asked for a continuance (delay) of the trial until the following Monday. It was not only because of the shortness of his preparation time; it was also because an influenza epidemic was raging in California and his 12-year-old daughter Margaret was seriously ill. A worldwide flu pandemic, one of the most lethal pandemics in modern history, had been claiming victims since 1918. Quinn denied the request, saying that the calendar had been set and the trial would start immediately. Potential jurors were questioned at some length, and that day and the next morning twelve of them, six men and six women, were chosen, along with a woman alternate.

Deputy District Attorney Myron Harris then outlined the prosecution's case in *People v. Whitney*. He took the jurors through the split in the Socialist Party and the creation first of the national Communist Labor Party and then of the California Communist Labor Party, saying the prosecution would show that the CLP was "for change by direct or industrial action, not by political action," and that Whitney was active in the Oakland convention. He also spoke about a song with lyrics of "Hurrah! Hurrah! We will make the Bolshevik victorious" that was sung during it. The convention "endorsed and adopted the soviet government of Russia" as well as the "seizing of private property by force," Harris charged, and the police had found radical literature and I.W.W. songs in Whitney's home. He accused Whitney of lying: "We will show that although she, herself, in expressions of opinion, may have said that she was for changes by political action, but that her every act . . . her every attitude and everything that she has done showed her to be a radical."

O'Connor moved to strike all of the opening statement that did not refer specifically to acts taken by Whitney. Pemberton joined in, objecting in addition, as he had in his unsuccessful pre-trial motions, that the California CLP's organizing events described by Harris had taken place on November 9 but that Whitney was charged with events occurring on November 28. Both objections were overruled. Pemberton renewed his motion the following day, knowing it would again be denied, but presumably wanting both to underscore the point to the jury and to put it on the record for an appeal. Defense counsel would continue to make the same objection throughout the trial.

The first witness for the prosecution was Edward Condon, the journalist who wrote the *Oakland Enquirer* article about the convention. He elaborated on the information in it and on what he had seen during the meeting. Calkins placed into evidence the song sung at the convention about making "the Bolshevik victorious," which set off a small commotion in the courtroom and elicited an objection from O'Connor on the grounds that there was no evidence that Whitney had sung, seen, or heard the song. Judge Quinn overruled the objection and the questioning moved on to the resolution that Whitney had offered on behalf of her committee. Oddly, Condon interrupted the proceedings to ask if he could speak to Detective Fenton Thompson. The request was denied, but the reason Condon wanted to confer with Thompson became clear later on.

Condon was on the stand all day. As witnesses are permitted to testify about what they saw and heard, the prosecution used his presence to enter evidence about all the resolutions introduced at the convention, much of the discussions during it, and the people who were present at it. O'Connor objected repeatedly, and futilely, that none of the testimony had anything to do with Whitney. At one point Calkins responded to the objection.

Mr. Calkins: Our point is that it has to do with the Communist Labor Party, Mr. O'Connor.

Mr. O'Connor: I understand that. But there is a woman named Anita Whitney on trial here, and not the Communist Labor Party. The Communist Labor Party is not on trial here and the Communist Labor Party, as such, is not on trial in any court.

As the trial continued, however, it became apparent that both the Communist Labor Party and the I.W.W. were on trial, and what happened to Whitney could be considered collateral damage. O'Connor objected to no avail when the prosecution entered the *Communist Manifesto* into evidence, arguing that there was no connection between it and Whitney. The same objection would be made, with as little success, throughout the trial, as the prosecution read into the record CLP and I.W.W. songs, pamphlets, and parts of books. "The only thing that I am protesting about is that they are dragging in a lot of things that Miss Whitney has had nothing to do with," O'Connor exclaimed at one point, "and I say to these gentlemen that there will be no objection to anything that has her name attached." Had the prosecution introduced only things to which Whitney's name was attached, it would have had very little evidence.

Condon recounted at length the names of people who had been at the convention and the content of their speeches, without being able to identify Whitney as having been present when the speeches were made. Calkins led Condon into a description of the rhetoric used at the convention about industrial unionism and praise for the I.W.W. Pemberton objected, saying "I would hate to be bound by some things that have been said by some people at conventions that I have attended."

Condon also described the way the American flag had been covered by a red cloth. That would lead to the trial's most dramatic moment, when O'Connor stood up to begin his cross-examination.

O'Connor asked Condon whether he had observed anything at the convention that he recognized as so criminal that he felt impelled to report it to the police. Condon initially answered that he had not. Pushed further, Condon replied that perhaps the draping of the American flag was illegal.

Q. (O'Connor) All right, we will come to the draping of the American flag. Do you know a man by the name of Fenton Thompson?

A. (Condon) I do, yes.

Q. Did Fenton Thompson ever tell you that a plant that he had at that meeting draped that flag?

A. He did, yes . . .

Q. In other words, then, the red flag that you talked about this morning as having been thrown over the American flag was placed there by a dupe that Fenton Thompson had in that convention. Is that the fact?

A. That is what he told me.

Condon said that Thompson had told him about the "dupe" two weeks after the convention and again on the morning of his testimony. O'Connor turned and asked Thompson to stand where the jury could see him. "Is this the man who told you that one of his men draped the American flag with a red banner?" he asked Condon. The answer: "It is." Pemberton interjected, "This is the same Fenton Thompson who swore to the complaint in this case, isn't it?"

The prosecution quickly backed away from the curious case of the red banner, agreeing that "the red banner does go out of this case at this time" (the "red banner," according to a journalist writing some years later, was actually a maroon cloth that had lain on the piano before it was moved to the bookcase) and asserting that Condon had never told the district attorneys about the subterfuge. O'Connor nonetheless went after Condon's credibility as a witness, asking him why he had failed to mention Thompson when he referred to the covered flag three times in his earlier testimony. "I didn't have an opportunity," Condon said. "Did you tell Judge Samuels about it when you testified before him" at the preliminary hearing? "I did not, no, sir . . . I was not asked."

Q. And unless I happen to ask you now, you never would have told the jury that that was a frame-up, and you would have permitted this little woman, if need be, to go to the penitentiary with that in your mind?

A. I would, yes—no, I would not, no.

Q. That is all.

A. Wait a minute—I would not have permitted it to go to the jury as I do not consider that that is an essential piece of evidence, myself, sending her to the penitentiary—that is not—the fact that the red flag was draped there by anybody doesn't indicate that she is guilty of criminal syndicalism any more than the mere fact that she stayed there after this flag was draped makes her no more guilty than it does me.

O'Connor asked Condon to tell the jury about every single thing, word, or act of Whitney's that he observed at the convention. Condon replied that he first noticed her when she gave the report of the Credentials Committee and remained in the room for the rest of the morning. There was a break for lunch, and he had not seen her in the afternoon until it was time for the Resolutions Committee to report, at which time she entered the hall.

Q. Up to this point... was there anything said or done by Miss Whitney which excited your especial interest as having been in violation of any law?

A. There was not, no, sir...

Q. Did you hear Anita Whitney that afternoon make any speech?

A. No, sir, I did not...

Q. And that is all that you can tell the jury as to the activities of Miss Whitney on that day?

A. That is.

Having led Condon to make O'Connor's case that Whitney could not be connected to many of the events that had taken place at the convention, the attorney permitted the young journalist to leave the stand.

The next witness was John C. Taylor, the CLP secretary. He had taken minutes during the convention, and Harris used them to show that Whitney had attended, that the convention adopted the resolution calling for "industrial organization" rather than merely for involvement in the political process, and that she was elected as an alternate to the state executive committee. Harris hoped to demonstrate that as an alternate Whitney remained an active member of the CLP leadership after what he saw as the subversive resolution had been adopted. That presumably would have justified the November 28 date in the indictment. Taylor testified that as an alternate, Whitney was not present at most executive committee meetings, but that she had attended one in early January 1920. O'Connor pointed out that Harris was asking about dates well after November 28.

In cross-examining Taylor, O'Connor was able to show that Taylor was under indictment himself and that Fenton Thompson had taken him to the district attorney's office a few days earlier to confer about his testimony. O'Connor tried to ask Taylor whether Taylor had ever heard Whitney advocate violence. Harris objected and Judge Quinn sustained the objection. O'Connor then used the language of each count of the indictment, asking Taylor whether he had ever known Whitney to do any of the acts listed in it. Harris objected repeatedly and again the judge ruled the questions out of order. "We want to show to this jury," O'Connor protested, "that never in her life did Anita Whitney ever say or do a single thing . . . which can even by the wildest flight of the imagination be constructed into an act of violence or a suggestion of violence. Now, how are we to prove it, your Honor, unless we take their own witness, the man they put upon the stand and the man who is associated . . . with Anita Whitney . . . and say to him, 'What did Miss Whitney do?' And the jury are entitled to know it, your Honor."

The judge was unimpressed. When Taylor nonetheless managed to get in "I never heard her say anything or have I seen her do anything that would bring her or make her guilty within this statute," Quinn ordered the remark stricken from the record. The court soon adjourned for the day and the jurors were led off to the Hotel Oakland, where they remained sequestered until the trial was over.

When court reconvened the next day, the prosecution returned to the red banner incident, putting Fenton Thompson on the stand to deny that he was involved in it. O'Connor objected that the prosecution could not call a witness (Thompson) to impeach another of its witnesses (Condon).

> Mr. Calkins: I had not the slightest idea that counsel would be unwilling to have the District Attorney put his cards on the table and show every bit of evidence in this case . . .

Mr. O'Connor: The cards should have been on the table yesterday afternoon, sir, before the gentleman left, which gave Mr. Thompson thirty-six or twenty-four hours to think over his testimony. It was Mr. Thompson's cue to come forth yesterday and say "That is a lie" and he stood there silent with not a word from him.

When Calkins finished with Thompson, it was the defense's turn to ask him questions. O'Connor, however, was not able to cross-examine him. Pemberton had told the court earlier that "Mr. O'Connor is a very sick man." O'Connor had come down with the flu and was running a temperature of 103 degrees. He was so hoarse that he asked for permission to delay the cross-examination until he was well enough to conduct it. The animosity between the defense and prosecution was evident in Calkins's objection: "Mr. O'Connor is able to make long speeches here. Why he should be unable to ask a few simple questions, I don't understand."

"I did not expect Mr. Calkins to treat me with any more courtesy than he has Miss Whitney," O'Connor croaked.

"No man in your condition of health could cross-examine a witness at this particular time," Judge Quinn agreed. Instead of the cross-examination, the court turned to the prosecution's next witnesses.

Harris called delegates at the Loring Hall convention to the stand and used their testimony to put both the California CLP and the national CLP's constitutions into the record, along with the national's Platform and Program. A CLP official told the court that Whitney had attended CLP executive committee meetings after November 9, and another testified that as the acts of the state convention had not been ratified by Local Oakland, they were not binding on Whitney.

By then O'Connor's illness was so severe and so obvious that the prosecution asked for an adjournment. It was Thursday afternoon and the court would have been in session for only two hours the following day, so the trial was recessed until Monday. On Monday O'Connor was too sick to be in the courtroom, and a doctor told the court that Lucille Stegman, one of the jurors, had been taken home with the flu. Anita Whitney had also come down with it. Pemberton asked for a week's continuance, by which time he expected O'Connor to return. "I am not charged with the responsibility of the trial in this case," he said.

"I came here Tuesday morning expecting to withdraw from the case because I had other work to do . . . he [O'Connor] requested me to remain"; but Whitney wanted O'Connor to be her chief lawyer. Calkins, no doubt delighted that the redoubtable O'Connor was out, accused Pemberton of false modesty and argued that a week's delay would be too burdensome for the jury. He suggested a continuance of two days, during which Whitney could look for another lawyer. Whitney immediately interrupted Calkins.

The Defendant: I should like to speak on this matter myself.

Mr. Pemberton: I request, your Honor, that she be allowed to speak.

The Court: I would rather have the counsel speak and take charge.

The Defendant: I do not consider that Mr. Pemberton is my counsel in my trial case, and any one who has sat through this last week in the court knows that Mr. O'Connor has charge of my case. I am an American citizen. I am not here to ask for sympathy. I am here to ask for justice, and you must remember that I am on trial for an offense which carries a penalty of fourteen years imprisonment. . . . Mr. O'Connor is an ill man, and I feel he will not be able to take charge of the case within two days.

Whitney showed Judge Quinn a letter from O'Connor's doctor attesting to the seriousness of the attorney's illness. Pemberton offered to let the jurors go home until the trial could be begun again, which would have released them from their confinement to the hotel and saved the county the expense of their food and lodging. Instead, Quinn adjourned the court until Wednesday morning. As he did so, he directed the officers of the court to change what had been their procedure, no longer permitting the public to take seats in front of the rail separating the public part of the courtroom from that of the participants. It would cut down on the number of people who could be admitted, but the judge was worried about infection and directed as well that the jurors have access to a doctor at all times.

Wednesday morning arrived but O'Connor did not. "We are unable to go on with the trial this morning," Pemberton told the judge. "Miss Whitney is herself still sick but able to be around, but coughing severely, and Mr. O'Connor—Mr. Harris, what did Mrs. O'Connor say in that regard?" Harris had spoken to O'Connor's wife on the telephone and learned that the lawyer was delirious. "She said that he was very much worried over the outcome of this case, and that she thought that a continuance of this case might relieve him mentally, at least." Pemberton reported that Whitney had tried but had been unable to get another lawyer, and "it is not [to] be wondered at, under the circumstances, for I doubt if any counsel . . . would think himself able to come in at this stage of the case and do justice to the defendant. . . . This case cannot be tried, considering the great responsibility involved, with justice to the defendant, without Mr. O'Connor's presence or without a very considerable time to allow another attorney to get in and take charge of the case." Pemberton added that Whitney did not consider him to be her lawyer.

That persuaded neither Calkins nor Judge Quinn. The judge was concerned that a continuance might last for some weeks, and Calkins refused to agree to a delay. "Give us one week," Pemberton pleaded. "We will consent that the jury may be dismissed from the care and charge of the sheriff." When Quinn refused, Whitney tried to interject.

The Defendant: Your Honor—
The Court: Just a minute—you have been represented by your counsel.
The Defendant: I am not represented by my counsel, your Honor.
The Court: You are represented, and you will proceed here by your counsel.
Mr. Pemberton: I withdraw from the case, if the Court please.
The Court: The Court will not permit you to withdraw at this time.

Quinn insisted that Pemberton continue; Pemberton insisted no less vigorously that Whitney did not want him to represent her. "May the Court please, may I have a few minutes to consult with Miss Whitney?" Pemberton finally begged. "I will go to jail before I will go on with this case without her consent." Quinn gave him ten minutes. When it was over, Pemberton reported that Whitney wished to speak to the court about a continuance. Quinn declined to hear her and ordered the trial to be resumed. The alternate juror was sworn in as a substitute for the still-ailing Lucille Stegman. Whitney, who did not want Pemberton jailed for contempt of court and had resigned herself to going on with the trial, began to take notes for him.

A police officer testified to seeing Whitney and other CLP members in the CLP office on dates in December and January and to removing "perhaps a ton" of "un-American" literature from it. Pemberton did not ask him why he considered it "un-American." Then court adjourned for the day. It was adjourned again the following day, Thursday, February 5, and again on Friday, because of the intestinal illness of another one of the jurors.

Whitney had gone to O'Connor's home in San Francisco at least once during his illness. The attorney had been adamant about his desire to cross-examine Fenton Thompson. Finally realizing that he would not return to the courtroom in time to do so, if at all, he recommended that the job be given to his fellow attorney Nathan C. Coghlan. Coghlan had unsuccessfully defended California Wobblies in 1919 from Espionage Act charges of sabotage and terrorism. He was in fact in Judge Quinn's courtroom on February 4, although he had not been formally added to the defense team, perhaps because Whitney had made it clear to O'Connor that Coghlan's less than outstanding career left her with no confidence in him. O'Connor therefore asked her to return to his home on Saturday, February 7, so that the ailing lawyer could give her the line of questioning Coghlan could use in cross-examining Thompson. Whitney left early that morning to take the ferry from Oakland to San Francisco. When the boat arrived at the pier, Whitney caught sight of a headline in the *San Francisco Examiner:* "O'Connor, Whitney Lawyer, Dead."

CHAPTER FOUR

The Trial Continues

Thomas O'Connor's death was foremost in the minds of all the participants when court reconvened on the morning of Monday, February 9. District Attorney Decoto himself appeared in court to join Pemberton in asking for an adjournment in honor of his late colleague's memory. Calling O'Connor a friend, Decoto described him as "one of the finest characters and one of the best lawyers" he had ever known. Judge Quinn was equally fulsome in his praise of O'Connor, lauding him as "one of the most lovable men" whose "personal and private life was as pure as the driven snow," and "a man of almost superhuman ability in the profession of the law." Whitney and some of the women jurors wept during the eulogies for O'Connor and for Lucille Stegman as well, for she, too, had died of the flu she contracted during the trial.

Before court adjourned for the day, Nathan Coghlan was formally recognized as having taken O'Connor's place as Whitney's attorney of record. Whitney would write bitterly about being forced to continue the trial with Coghlan, who came in "without any opportunity for preparation," and Pemberton, who had "declared himself both unwilling and incompetent" to handle the case. Zechariah Chafee and other scholars have speculated that the trial might have ended very differently had O'Connor not died. Whether or not that is correct, it is certain that what ensued was a mockery of due process. Coghlan presumably did his best. It was not sufficient.

The trial began once again on the morning of Tuesday, February 10, and continued through Friday, February 20. The goal of the prosecutors, judging from their choice of witnesses and exhibits throughout the remainder of the trial, was to connect Whitney with the worst excesses of the I.W.W. Calkin and Harris first had to establish that Whitney was a member of the California Communist Labor Party, which was simple enough; she made no bones about that. Then they wanted to show that the party, as exemplified by the founding state convention at Loring Hall, was an antigovernment conspiracy. As the alleged secret criminal conspiracy to overthrow the government took place at a public convention to which the press was invited, the convention itself was poor proof. The nefarious purposes of the CLP had to be demonstrated by other means, and so the prosecution chose to link the party to the much-hated Wobblies. The California CLP had existed for such a short time before it was effectively put out of business by the police raid and subsequent prosecutions, however, that it had no institutional links to the Wobblies or any other entity at all. The way to get around that was to argue that the state party was connected to the national party, which in turn could be shown to be sympathetic to the Wobblies.

The California CLP had adopted the platform of the national party. One paragraph in the national platform read: "In any mention of revolutionary industrial unionism in this country, there must be recognition of the immense effect upon the American labor movement of the Industrial Workers of the World, whose long and valiant struggles and heroic sacrifices in the class-war have earned the respect and affection of all workers everywhere. We greet the revolutionary industrial proletariat of America and pledge them our wholehearted support and cooperation in their struggles against the capitalist class." On the basis of that paragraph, Judge Quinn, whose rulings throughout the trial favored the prosecution and violated the norms of due process, allowed the prosecution to introduce pages and pages of evidence about the nature and activities of the I.W.W.

If Wobbly activities seem somewhat remote from anything Whitney herself did, that is because they were, but the prosecution was determined to convict her by any means necessary. Whitney had of course not been at the national party convention. Whitney was not a member of the I.W.W. Whitney could not be tied to any publication or act aimed at overthrow of the government. So, with the acquiescence of the judge presiding over the case, the prosecutors metaphorically and in one instance literally dragged into the courtroom both the I.W.W. itself and any law-breaking Wobblies they could find.

———

The obvious question is why the county bothered prosecuting Whitney at all. Part of the answer lies in the context of the trials of other CLP and I.W.W. members taking place in California during the same time period.

The California criminal syndicalism law went into effect on April 30, 1919. By the end of that year 108 people had been indicted under it, charged with membership in the CLP (or the Socialist Party before it—remember that the California Socialist Party did not turn itself into the CLP until November of that year) or the I.W.W. or both. Between 1919 and 1924, when enforcement efforts stopped, 531 Californians were charged with violating the act. Only 164 were convicted, and almost half of the convictions appealed to a higher court were overturned—presumably because the proceedings in the trial courts, like the Whitney court, were so shoddy. It is hard to escape the conclusion that both prosecutors and trial court judges were infected with the anti–I.W.W. hysteria that seized the western states in the postwar era.

The Whitney prosecution both relied on a template that had already been established and reinforced the likelihood of its use in future prosecutions. By the time Whitney's trial began, as mentioned earlier, Judge Quinn had presided over the trial of James McHugo, a Wobbly organizer, and sentenced him to one to fourteen years in prison. Elbert Coutts and John Dymond, former Wobbly leaders who had become and would continue to be witnesses in criminal syndicalism cases, testified in the McHugo trial and would do so in half a dozen other such cases as well as Whitney's. Fenton Thompson had also testified in the McHugo trial. The lead prosecutor in both cases was John Calkins. Judge Quinn ran the McHugo case and others that followed it as he would the Whitney trial, permitting it to be about the I.W.W. rather than any acts of the accused person, denying defense motions to have the specifics of the charges articulated, and allowing substantial hearsay evidence. Prosecutors throughout California, including the Oakland district attorney's office, followed a similar playbook in fashioning criminal syndicalism cases such as Whitney's. They included all five charges under the law in the indictments—organizing, writing, advocating, publishing, teaching—but rarely attempted during trial to prove anything beyond the crime of participating in organizing or being a member in an organization devoted to violence. The multiplicity of charges that the prosecutors had no intention of proving was seemingly designed to make the jury believe that anyone accused of so many things must surely have been guilty of something.

That still leaves the question of why Whitney was charged. Fenton Thompson had clearly been gunning for her and other CLP members. (Rightly or wrongly, Whitney believed that Thompson had a special animus against her. She told her attorney that a Wobbly serving time in San Quentin had been promised immunity by Thompson if he would testify to seeing her at "an orgy" in Berkeley.) It was no secret that Thompson had been putting together information about the I.W.W. for some time, but while Oakland prosecutors may have decided to charge Whitney as a way of providing themselves with what was certain to be a well-publicized platform, it is hard to believe that they really considered her a danger to the state of California. She may have been chosen for prosecution precisely for that reason. If the Wobblies could be shown to have ensnared even such a well-known model of upstanding citizenship, such a pillar of society, their danger presumably was all the greater than if their members were merely the far less "respectable" migrant workers.

And so, following their playbook, the prosecutors continued to put the I.W.W. on trial. John Dymond had been the Fresno I.W.W. secretary for two months in 1918, handling I.W.W. publications, and Harris used Dymond's former position as the occasion for reading lengthy excerpts from I.W.W. publications into the trial record over the next few days. The defense's repeated objections that none of the publications was shown to have any connection to Whitney were overruled. The publications included incendiary works such as Elizabeth Gurley Flynn's *Sabotage* and Big Bill Haywood's *The General Strikes*. The prosecution also put into evidence and read from a number of left-wing works on sabotage—Earl C. Ford and William Z. Foster's *Syndicalism* and Walker C. Smith's *Sabotage*, for example—that were not I.W.W. publications but that, Dymond testified, were circulated by the organization. All the publications advocated strikes and sabotage, particularly of machinery. Later in the trial the prosecution introduced additional Wobbly publications, including a parody of "Onward, Christian Soldiers" from the *Joe Hill Memorial Edition of I.W.W. Songs*. The parody included lines like "Onward, Christian soldiers, rip and tear and smite; Let the gentle Jesus, bless your dynamite" and "Onward, Christian soldiers! Drench the land with gore; Mercy is a weakness all the gods abhor. Bayonet the babies, jab the mothers, too; Hoist the cross of Calvary to hallow all you do." One can imagine the faces of the offended jurors, who nonetheless may have considered that reading and the reading of other Wobbly songs, which take up seven pages of the trial transcript, to be a relief from the turgid prose of the books and pamphlets. Whatever their reaction, Whitney was now painted by extension not only as radical but unchristian.

Coghlan's cross-examination did what it could to mitigate the impact of Dymond's testimony. He had Dymond admit that he had become an informer in 1918. Dymond had testified that the Wobblies' Tenth Convention had advocated sabotage, which he said included "tell[ing] the truth as to what actually transpired in these industries," "sowing Johnson grass or Bermuda grass, or other destructive grasses, in orchards or vineyards," and using emery dust to destroy machinery. Coghlan then read from the Tenth Convention proceedings, to show that nothing in them actually advocated sabotage. The prosecution's tactic of putting the Wobblies on trial had in effect landed Coghlan in the uncomfortable position of demonstrating that they really weren't so bad, after all. More positively, he managed to get Dymond to distance Whitney from the I.W.W.

Q. And you know that this lady never held a card in your organization, don't you?

A. I do, yes.

Q. And you know she did not?

A. I know she did not, yes.

Q. And that she had nothing to do with this resolution or with any other resolution of that kind with relation . . . either to sabotage or any other matter presented to your general convention, as indicated by this book.

A. I know she had nothing to do with any of the proceedings in the Tenth Convention; yes.

All of that took place on February 10. Fenton Thompson was scheduled for cross-examination as soon as the trial reconvened but was excused because Coghlan had not had a chance to read his testimony. In fact, Coghlan apparently decided that no purpose would be served by calling Thompson to the stand, and the trial would end without the police officer speaking again.

The following day, Wednesday, February 11, Whitney arrived late because of illness. The *San Francisco Chronicle* reported that she was "very pale and she staggered slightly as she took her seat," and on Thursday she clearly had symptoms of the flu. Calkins was also out ill, and on other days illness kept Harris at home. Health problems were so rampant during the trial that the *Chronicle* began calling it the "Hoodoo Trial" and at one point was able to announce triumphantly, "Today was distinguished as one of the few days of the trial in which no one connected with the case was absent on account of sickness."

Elbert Coutts was called to testify about the production and distribution of I.W.W. "stickerettes," meant to be pasted on store windows and automobiles. They called for the freeing of Richard Ford and Herman Suhr, the two men convicted of murder following the Wheatland Hops riot. Presumably the prosecution wanted the jury to hear that the Wobblies attempted to free murderers. Coutts was then asked about other measures taken against hops growers in retaliation for the jailing. He reported that one I.W.W. official had said at a meeting that he favored burning hops kilns and "if it was necessary, they would burn up the whole state of California." There was no indication that Whitney had been anywhere near the meeting, known the official, known of his remarks, or favored arson, or that the Communist Labor Party had done so, but Whitney was now connected to arsonists as well as mockers of Christianity.

She was also about to be tried for the acts of people she did not know. Coutts was asked if he knew Robert "Dublin Bob" Kinellan, who was an I.W.W. "cat," or saboteur. An exasperated Coghlan demanded, "Do you connect, or show, that this lady was acquainted with Robert Kinellan?" Harris replied, "I think not, Mr. Coghlan. But we do expect to show that she was acquainted with others who were associated with Kinellan in doing certain work." Harris's statement was a remarkable instance of guilt by association. The "others" were never identified. Coutts then testified that he had made an electric furnace in Oakland that was supposed to produce phosphorus, which would be used to set fires to barns and haystacks. To what appeared to be the surprise of Harris, he added that the furnace didn't work.

> Mr. Pemberton: Do you claim that Miss Whitney knew anything about that, or ever heard of it?
>
> Mr. Harris: I don't know. But her friend, Miss Pollock, was there when it was being discussed.

Theodora Pollock was an acknowledged officer of the Wobblies. While she had argued against any organizational involvement in violence, she was one of the Wobblies found guilty under the Espionage Act when Coghlan defended her during the 1919 trial mentioned earlier. What she did or did not do, however, demonstrated nothing about Whitney.

Coutts then described setting barns and haystacks on fire, using sulphuric acid and cyanide of potassium to poison cattle, and putting lye in the shoes of people who would not join the I.W.W. Harris asked him if he had ever sold I.W.W. literature and used his reply, that he had, to read into the record yet more from Wobbly publications. Coghlan kept protesting the introduction of evidence about the Wobblies; Harris countered that it was relevant.

> Mr. Harris: I think that we are entitled to show any interest that she has in the I.W.W. organization . . . the testimony of the witness Coutts and Dymond [shows] the I.W.W. activities and the Example and Propaganda of that organization, and following that, we have the Communist Labor Party greeting it, as they say, "We greet the revolutionary industrial proletariat of America, and pledge them our whole-hearted support and co-operation in their struggle against the capitalist class."
>
> Mr. Coghlan: Your Honor will remember that that resolution which was imported into the proceedings of the local organization, of which this lady has been proven to be a member, that that resolution was opposed by Miss Whitney and passed over her consent and against her vote. . . . As your Honor knows . . . at a convention of any political party, there are innumerable resolutions that you or I might oppose in the passage of them . . . that does not itself

bind criminally upon a person charged with advocating in person the commission of crime.

Coghlan reminded the court that the CLP resolution Whitney proposed was for political involvement. Harris countered that the resolution "does not say that political action is to be the only action, it only speaks of the value of political action. . . . There isn't one place in the resolution wherein or whereby they condemn sabotage, condemn industrial change by force or violence."

> Mr. Coghlan: There isn't anything in the platform of the Republican or Democratic Party that condemns sabotage, but we all condemn it. . . . You cannot denounce this woman for what she did not say. . . . And if you are now going to use this as a bridge, as you have referred to it, upon which to convey over the testimony that you offer from these witnesses, repudiated members, even, of the I.W.W. and informers, why, it seems to me that that is traveling entirely outside of any known principle of evidence.

Harris replied that he would follow up with proof of illicit activity on Whitney's part and Judge Quinn overruled Coghlan's objection. No evidence of such activity, however, was ever introduced.

The trial continued in that vein, with even Judge Quinn protesting at one point that "we have the Communist Labor Party here on trial rather than the I.W.W. organization." (It was a bit of a strange comment, as presumably it was Whitney, not the CLP, who was accused of a crime.) He continued to allow questions about I.W.W. activities, however. Pemberton said at another moment that "as a gentleman of the press expressed it to me here this morning, you are trying this defendant for being obnoxious to the Police Department of Oakland." He once again requested specifics of the charges, pointing to California cases requiring that charges had to be specified. Exactly what publications, he asked, of the dozens that were put into evidence, was Whitney accused of being involved with? What subversive speeches was she accused of having given? The judge denied the request.

The prosecution rested, and the defense presented its only witness, Anita Whitney herself. Coghlan had her testify about her activities at the CLP's founding convention—her attendance there, her membership in the Resolutions Committee. What, he inquired, was the purpose of the convention?

Q. Was it to be, or did you intend that it should be an instrument of terrorism?
A. No, sir.
Q. Or of violence?
A. No, sir. . . .
Q. Did you or did you not know whether or not it was the purpose of that meeting to violate any known law?
A. I knew it was not. The meeting was an open convention . . . and would not, of course, have been an open convention if we were deliberately planning to break the laws of the State in which we live.

Coghlan ended his questioning. Whitney's direct testimony takes up less than two pages of a transcript that runs to hundreds of pages, presumably because Coghlan did not want to open the door for questioning by the prosecution about anything other than the convention. Then it was Harris's turn to examine Whitney.

His questioning resulted in very little testimony from Whitney and a great deal of jockeying among the lawyers about what was and was not proper cross-examination. First, however, Harris asked whether she had submitted a resolution to the convention "to the effect that you would use all force that was possible to free class war and political prisoners?" That was of course not what the resolution said. Harris read it aloud "to refresh your recollection," and the courtroom heard that the resolution called for the CLP to "use all its strength and energy in the organization and education of the workers to utilize to the full extent their collective power to force the unconditional release of each and every one now serving a sentence as a political or class war prisoner." "May I call the attention of the jury," Whitney interjected, "to the fact that resolution does not say that we will use force to free these prisoners but that we will use all our strength and energy to do so."

What Harris was after, however, was the idea of "class war prisoner." He asked Whitney whether she knew Herbert Stredwick, "the I.W.W. in

Fort Leavenworth [prison]" and considered him "a class war or a political prisoner?" Whitney replied after a lengthy colloquy between the lawyers about whether or not the question was proper cross-examination, and it became apparent that she had no intention of answering directly. Her attorneys apparently had told her to confine her testimony to the events at the convention.

> Whitney: I would say that at the time the resolution was drafted, as far as I know, no individuals were in the minds of any of the Committee, and certainly no names were mentioned on the adoption of this resolution.

Harris insisted on a reply, and she answered, "I did not have the man in mind at all at the time of the framing of the resolution." Harris asked if she knew other Wobblies convicted of crimes, and she replied that she had corresponded with some of them. Harris questioned her about other jailed I.W.W. members and whether she considered them to be class war prisoners. Whitney repeatedly answered that she did not have them in mind when the resolution was drawn up. Still intent on connecting Whitney to the I.W.W., Harris inquired:

> Q. At the time that you drew up this resolution, did you consider any I.W.W.'s as class war prisoners?
> A. I can't say that I took that matter into consideration whatsoever.
> Q. You had sent $5 to the I.W.W. Defense fund for the defense of the I.W.W.'s who were class war prisoners; that is, sent it to Bill Haywood, had you not?

Coghlan objected, but, undeterred, Harris asked again, "whom you considered to be class war prisoners in drawing up that resolution. . . . You meant men who had a violation of the law as class war prisoners?"

> A. I should not consider class war prisoners necessarily men that had broken any law. I should say a class war prisoner was a person who was in jail in an attempt to better the working conditions of men and the families of working men.
> Q. And charged with a violation of what law, please? . . .

A. I do not think that I could mention any specific law.

Q. You mean the Espionage Act for instance, or refusal to go to war?

A. No; I said that I considered class war prisoners men or women who were in jail for an attempt to better the conditions of the working men and their families and children.

Q. For instance, Ford and Suhr, who were in jail to better conditions, as you call it, who murdered a man in Yolo County . . . who are in the penitentiary at Folsom? . . . We know very well that people are not in jail for bettering conditions.

Mr. Coghlan: I don't know about that . . . I think that is what you put her in jail for, or attempted to.

Harris kept pounding away at whom Whitney considered to be a class war prisoner, and she finally named Eugene Debs and Kate Richards O'Hare. "What was Eugene Debs charged with, if you know?" Harris demanded. "I will ask you is it not a fact that he was charged with a violation of the Espionage Act? . . . Kate Richards O'Hare was arrested and convicted by a jury in the United States Court for obstructing the draft of men into the United States Army, to fight with Germany, was she not?" Judge Quinn finally sustained Coghlan's objections that Whitney's view of Debs and O'Hare had nothing to do with whether or not she advocated criminal syndicalism and that the questions were not appropriate cross-examination. He did permit Harris to ask whom else Whitney thought of as class war prisoners.

A. I have tried to make it plain that I had not formulated a list of class war prisoners. I drew up, helped to draw up a resolution which was presented to the Communist Labor Party of California, and it is then for them to define whom the Party considers as class war prisoners or political prisoners.

Harris went back to asking whether Whitney considered other specific convicted I.W.W. members to be class war prisoners, and Whitney replied, "I am not prepared to name any others." The judge reminded Harris that the only appropriate questions had to do with anything intended at the time of the passage of the resolution, but the prosecutor had already brought a laundry list of convicted Wobblies to the attention of the jury. Harris asked if Whitney considered people prosecuted under the criminal syndicalism law to be class war prisoners and she answered, "Not necessarily."

Coghlan took over for redirect examination.

> Mr. Coghlan: You have in mind, have you or have you not, a present subsisting example of what you deem to be class war imprisonment? . . . What is that example?
>
> A. Well, I think I can name some of the cases of the people who have been arrested under the criminal syndicalist law.

The lawyers wrangled again about what could be asked, and Coghlan turned instead to the resolution itself, getting Whitney to say one last time that neither the resolution nor the people present at the convention intended to violate the laws. The defense then rested.

The prosecution and defense presented their closing arguments on February 20. Harris used the occasion to return to the red cloth placed over the American flag during the Loring Hall convention. First he castigated the police department, telling the jury that "if the police department were instrumental in placing that flag there, there is no censure too severe for them." Then, however, he moved the blame from the police to Whitney.

> If you were there, or if I were there, and our "Old Glory" as she stands was covered by that dirty red rag, what would you have done, or what would I have done? I would have yanked it off from the face of that American flag and thrown it into the street. . . . But did Anita Whitney do that? . . . Not for a single minute, ladies and gentlemen of the jury, not for one minute did Anita Whitney do that which you and I have been brought up to do, namely, to revere and honor that flag that stands for us, and speaks for our freedom and love of country.

Coghlan would counter that the red flag incident demonstrated the "artificial" nature of the charges. Harris and Calkins's summations continued the tactic of turning the trial into a referendum on the I.W.W. Coghlan in turn reminded the jury that the only two resolutions presented to the national Communist Labor Party by the I.W.W. had been rejected. Harris questioned that. The CLP had endorsed the Third Manifesto, he said. "In this action and in other actions, the record of the Communist Labor Party and the Industrial Workers of the World is parallel." Calkins added, "The Communist Labor Party of America is but a political adjunct of the Industrial Workers of the World. . . . It is bound with chains and brass to the I.W.W. and forms for them a political unit through which they hope to seize the political as well as the industrial control of this country." What the jury had to do, Harris added in a two-hour oration, was "uphold the sacred tenets of Americanism" and come in with a verdict that would set "the seal of disapproval on the activities of the Communist Labor Party and its blood brother, the I.W.W." He then made the object of the trial quite clear: "It is not only Anita Whitney on trial, but the dark doctrines of envy, murder and terror." According to the *Oakland Tribune*, "So eloquent was the concluding address and so well had Harris illustrated the principles at stake that several of the jurors were moved to tears."

Judge Quinn charged the jury and sent it out to deliberate at 4:50 on the afternoon of February 20. The jurors filed into the courtroom at 9:30 that evening to say that they could not reach agreement on all the counts and were uncertain what to do. Quinn sent them back at 9:43 after instructing that they could come in with a verdict on only one or more counts if they could not reach agreement on all of them. They returned at 10:42 to announce that they were still deadlocked on four counts but finally had agreed on one: Anita Whitney was guilty of organizing or helping to organize an organization designed to "advocate, teach or aid and abet criminal syndicalism."

Judge Quinn promptly sent Whitney off to the county jail. He would hand down her sentence on February 24.

It seemed clear that the prosecution's tactic of putting the I.W.W. rather than Whitney on trial was successful. One juror told the *San Francisco Chronicle* that while "'there was not sufficient evidence to support some of the charges,'" a blanket acquittal "would have been equivalent to saying that the jury sanctioned the I.W.W. and the Communist Labor Party and believed them to be lawful, worthy organizations."

The jurors were thanked and allowed to go home. Tedious and confusing as the trial may have been for them—one juror repeatedly complained that he did not know what was going on—they apparently did not suffer greatly from being sequestered. The trial concluded twenty-four days after it began. That is when the press discovered and reported with outrage that the bill for the jurors' expenses came to $3,000, which included the costs of cigarettes, candy, magazines, chewing gum, 742 cigars, 14 haircuts, and 47 shaves, in addition to room and board.

When Anita Whitney entered Judge Quinn's courtroom on the mild, sunny afternoon of February 24, dozens of her supporters rose to their feet. Many but not all of them were women; many worked in social service and welfare agencies. They remained standing until Whitney took her seat. Judge Quinn pronounced sentence: as the criminal syndicalism law specified for anyone convicted under it, Whitney was to be held in San Quentin state prison for from one to fourteen years.

The *Oakland Tribune* reported that Whitney "plainly showed the effects of her incarceration and appeared to be controlling herself with difficulty." Her supporters were less restrained; some of them, weeping, rushed up to embrace her. The sheriff of Alameda County was directed to turn her over to the warden of San Quentin, but Quinn delayed execution of the sentence for ten days so that Coghlan could file an appeal with the District Court of Appeal, and Whitney was returned to the county jail. Quinn denied requests for bail both from Whitney herself and from a number of people prepared to post bond for her. Within weeks, he and Calkins had moved on to trials of other CLP members.

The furor over Whitney, however, continued unabated. Her sympathizers went to the county jail regularly in the hope of seeing her. Some women with quite another view reportedly threatened to tar and feather her if she was released, and Myron Harris ordered deputy sheriffs to guard Whitney whenever she was taken to court during her continued requests for bail. An extraordinary array of prominent citizens, including the state senator who had introduced the criminal syndicalism act; Dean Gresham, of Grace Cathedral; Edward Hanna, the archbishop of San Francisco; Rabbi Martin A. Meyer, of Temple Emanu-El; the vice president of the Council of Catholic Women; and university professors signed petitions calling for her to be released on bail. The *San Francisco Monitor*, the official organ of the San Francisco Catholic archdiocese, which carried an article blasting the conviction and calling her "a noble and beautiful character" and a "gentle woman of peace and charity," characterized the conviction as the result of "un-American hysteria and illiberalism." The sentiment was not unanimous. With the misogynous fervor that seems to have characterized much of the anti-Whitney sentiment, the *Sacramento Bee* opined that Whitney "has prostituted her talents for years to the service of the lawless and disorderly" and that "the female of the species is more deadly than the male."

Deadly traitor or innocent victim, Whitney was about to leave jail. On March 1, Judge Quinn granted bail after three prominent physicians reported that she suffered from low-grade anemia and chronic endocarditis, an inflammation of the heart valves. They added that she had had minor operations over the last year and a half as well as bronchial ailments and possible tuberculosis, and that her pulse, blood, and temperature readings were subnormal. Continued confinement, they testified, would threaten her health. The district attorney's office did not contest the plea. A former city commissioner of Oakland and the president of Associated Charities posted $10,000 in Liberty bonds, and Whitney walked out of jail to the hugs of admirers and bouquets of flowers.

Whitney had seemed serene during her imprisonment. "Why should I not be calm and happy?" she said to a journalist who reported on an interview in the *New York Times*. "I feel that I have done no wrong. . . . I would have been a coward" if she had not stood up for what she believed. "My father always taught me to stand up to things—to judge for myself the difference between right and wrong . . . the greatest satisfaction in life comes from obeying your own conscience and helping in your own small way to make the world a little better for someone else because you have lived." It was her conscience that compelled her to write an article for *The Survey* magazine about the conditions in the women's section of the county jail. She slept in cell number three on what she called "an iron gridiron, on which was placed a thin mattress" that left her hips sore. Papers and magazines were forbidden, but friends managed to smuggle some in, and she used those to line the "bed." Her cellmate was a prostitute who Whitney suspected had a venereal disease but with whom she had to share an open toilet and a washstand with running cold water. The two of them and other prisoners, including yet another woman with a "social disease," washed their clothes in a common galvanized tub. One fellow prisoner was a drug addict whom the prison doctor hoped to wean by administering constantly smaller doses of drugs. The doses were not large enough to cushion the withdrawal, and "when the nervousness became unbearable," the woman would tear an opening in her leg and inject herself with a mixture of tobacco and water to ease the pain. Meals were mostly starch: potatoes, rice, macaroni, beans, bread—although the clearly sympathetic jailers allowed Whitney, but no one else, to keep fruit brought in by friends. "Thus does the state treat its erring citizens," Whitney wrote indignantly. "The system is vengeful, merciless, and needlessly ignorant of the source of crime and human needs. Are we building up hate? Then, must we reap the whirlwind?"

For at least the moment, though, Whitney was away from the horrors of jail. Now her fate was up to the appellate courts. She was 53 years old. She would be 60 before her case finally ended.

The first court to which a person convicted in a California Superior Court can turn is the District Court of Appeal. Each geographic area of California has one, and the court with jurisdiction over Oakland was the First District Court of Appeal. The California constitution requires District Courts of Appeal to look for procedural errors; they do not hear testimony or examine the jury's factual findings. Coghlan and Pemberton therefore appealed on a multiplicity of procedural grounds, including that Whitney had never been told the specifics of the charges against her, she was denied the right to be represented by herself or by the lawyer of her choice, the evidence did not support the conviction, there was nothing in the record to show that the CLP advocated criminal syndicalism, she had no personal knowledge of any syndicalist intentions or activities of the CLP and, importantly, the introduction of testimony about the I.W.W. prejudiced her case. They referred as well to the privileges and immunities clause of the federal Constitution's Fourteenth Amendment ("No state shall make or enforce any law which shall abridge the privileges or immunities of citizens of the United States"), arguing that one of those privileges was the right to join political organizations such as the Communist Labor Party. They also claimed that the syndicalism law violated the Fourteenth Amendment's due process and equal protection clauses ("No state shall . . . deprive any person of life, liberty, or property, without due process of law; nor deny to any person within its jurisdiction the equal protection of the laws.").

The appeal was filed on February 28, 1920. There is no indication of why the District Court of Appeal took so long with the case, but it did not hand down its decision until April 25, 1922. In the interim, Whitney acquired a new lawyer.

John Francis Neylan was a California newspaper reporter and publisher, as well as an attorney for and advisor to William Randolph Hearst. He was a firm opponent of communists and other left-wingers, and considered the Wobblies "a terrible outfit." The well-connected Neylan had clashed with Whitney when he was running the State Board of Control, which supervised charitable institutions in California, and thought her a bit of a crank. When Archbishop Hanna, Rabbi Meyer, and the Reverend Charles Lathrop asked him to handle Whitney's appeal, he declined, saying he knew nothing about criminal law and "Besides, I don't know why I should go out of my way for Miss Whitney." He was nonetheless persuaded to look at the transcript of Whitney's trial and was so outraged by what he saw as the "most flagrant, shameful abuse of the legal process" that he agreed to take on her case without fee. Neylan tried to get other lawyers to join him, but they all refused to be identified with the case. "You want to remember that feeling was running pretty high against criminal syndicalism," he later told an interviewer.

His entry into the case did not produce immediate results. The decision finally issued by the three-judge panel of the District Court of Appeal affirmed Whitney's conviction. Whitney's contention that the indictment did not mention the organization to which she was accused of belonging failed, the court said, because the CLP had been mentioned during the district attorney's opening statement and because the state supreme court had held that it was sufficient for criminal syndicalism indictments to include no more than the language of the statute. Evidence about the I.W.W. was properly introduced, Judge John E. Richards wrote for the court, because it tended to show "the character and purposes of the Communist Labor Party of California." Finally, the court castigated Whitney for claiming not to believe that the CLP was a syndicalist organization. "That this defendant did not realize that she was giving herself over to forms and expressions of disloyalty and was, to say the least of it, lending her presence and the influence of her character and position as a woman of refinement and culture to an organization whose purposes and sympathies savored of treason," Richards held, was "past belief." Once again, Whitney was seemingly damned for providing a veneer of respectability to a despised organization—and, perhaps, for being female.

The next step was an appeal to the California Supreme Court, which had the discretion to hear or decline to hear the case. The court declined, and on June 3, 1922, Neylan filed a petition for rehearing. Those who think that all lawyers' briefs consist of no more than dry citations might be surprised at Neylan's prose. "The appellant believes," he wrote, "that no intelligent human being can review the record of her trial and not be forced to believe that a conviction was secured by inflaming the minds of the jurors with the idea that she was in some degree responsible for and sympathetic with the atrocious crimes committed either by these organizations [the I.W.W. or Russian Bolsheviks] or members thereof." An analysis of all the testimony

> does not disclose one word purporting to show: That she ever committed an act of violence; That she ever aided or abetted violence; That she ever advised violence; That she ever uttered a violent sentence; That she ever knew of any act of violence . . . by any organization or individual belonging to any organization; Or even that the organization in which she admits membership ever committed any act of violence. . . . On the contrary, the record indicates that Charlotte Anita Whitney was opposed to all violence and held convictions against it as strongly as those held by people of the Quaker faith.

Neylan fulminated that

> never in the history of California was there a plainer miscarriage of justice. Never in the history of California was a defendant before a court of justice so ruthlessly deprived of vital rights guaranteed under the Constitution. Never was there a more apparent indecent haste to appease public wrath by the offering up of a vicarious sacrifice. . . . The transcript of testimony shows that conservatively speaking, sixty per cent of the testimony taken had reference to the

Bolshevists of Russia or the acts of I.W.W.'s. To assert that this testimony did not arouse in the jury an unjust prejudice against the defendant after the jury had witnessed the admission of this testimony as pertinent, competent and relevant and after the jury had listened to this testimony hour after hour and day after day, is to deny the obvious.

The court was unconvinced and again refused to hear the case. It appeared that Whitney would go to San Quentin. Speaking with a reporter, she sounded both resigned and still firmly committed to her principles. "I am not whimpering at my sentence," she said. "It may be terrible for me, it has been worse for others. . . . I have been in the women's section there [San Quentin], and it is horrible." Still, "I go without retrenching one bit upon the platform of my life." Whitney called the Declaration of Independence "the finest rule of life we have." She read it as saying, "To all people an equal opportunity," meaning that "men should not struggle for decent hours and a decent wage . . . children should be born with health and a chance for happiness, and . . . women should be granted the privilege of decent working hours and plenty of rest and decent pay." "Can anything be greater than that?" she asked.

There was still one faint hope that Whitney might be able to avoid San Quentin. It lay with the Supreme Court of the United States, and Neylan immediately announced that he would file a petition asking it to review the decision. The reason the hope was merely faint was that the Supreme Court would review a criminal conviction from state courts only if the attorneys could claim that the actions of those courts violated a federal statute or the federal constitution. The District Court of Appeal had not mentioned the federal constitution or Whitney's constitutional rights under it. Neylan's brief for the high court nonetheless argued that the District Court of Appeal *should* have decided that the criminal syndicalism act violated the Fourteenth Amendment to the Constitution, and cited the amendment's provisions about due process and equal protection. The California law penalized speech by people who advocated change in the industrial or political system but permitted speech by those advocating the status quo: that was a violation of the equal protection clause. In addition, Whitney was deprived of due process at trial because she was not told the specifics of the charges against her. As to the prosecution's insistence that the CLP endorsed the I.W.W., Neylan exclaimed, "It would be as logical to say that the execution of a treaty with Great Britain by the Republic of Liberia would be a Liberian endorsement of the murder of the Romanoff family by the Russian Reds because Great Britain has recognized the Soviet Government."

After hearing oral argument, the Supreme Court declared on October 19, 1925, that it would not decide the case. The court lacked jurisdiction because there had been no reference to the Constitution or federal statutes in the District Court of Appeal's opinion.

The press exploded with comments from partisans on both sides. "Patriotic Citizens Deplore Martyrdom of Gentle Woman," Hearst's *San Francisco Call* trumpeted. That provoked an outraged response from the *Sacramento Bee*: "*The Bee* takes the attitude that such citizens are hardly patriotic and that the woman is not exactly gentle . . . the 'gentle' woman whose purse-strings have yielded the sinews of war for the I.W.W. for years past." William Locke, one of the California legislators involved in passing the syndicalism law, declared that it "was never intended to halt free speech nor to punish persons for their thoughts" and worried that imprisoning Whitney "will make her a martyr in the eyes of the radical element." The *Baltimore Sun* charged that there was something "obviously rotten" in the state of California if Whitney was sent back to jail, and the *New York World* added that imprisoning her would demonstrate that "our liberties are at a low ebb, indeed." The *Mobile Register*, however, warned that "persons who do not want to be branded as Reds should stay out of Red company" and the *Des Moines Register* quoted the editor of the *Iowa Legionnaire* as commenting, "It is amusing to see these traitors who advocate the overthrow of our Government by force, when convicted, come bawling to public sentiment for support in their pleas for mercy from the same courts they have scoffed at."

A major campaign to pardon Whitney sprang up. Some of Harvard Law School's most notable professors, Felix Frankfurter and Zechariah Chafee among them, called for California governor Friend W. Richardson to pardon her. So did the deans of the law schools at University of California–Berkeley and Columbia University; the presidents of Wellesley, Smith, Vassar, Mills, and Swarthmore Colleges; former U.S. senator James D. Phelan; San Francisco district attorney Matthew

Brady; novelist Upton Sinclair; social worker Jane Addams; the executive board of the California Women's Christian Temperance Union; former Berkeley mayor Louis Bartlett; a former justice of the state supreme court; the Episcopal bishop of California; William Kehoe; and thousands of others. Frankfurter issued a call for "those who believe in a liberal interpretation of civil rights" to write to Richardson. The American Civil Liberties Union announced a nationwide campaign to free Whitney, and the organization's California branch sent a delegation to meet with the governor.

Whitney herself refused to join the effort. "I must abide by the decision," she told the press. "In what I did I was taking the constitution of the United States at its word when it comes to the guarantee of free speech. I believed then that I was within my constitutional rights, and I believe now that I was. . . . I am not going to ask for a pardon. If the Governor is disposed to pardon any one," she said, remaining true to her egalitarian principles, "let him liberate the poor men who are now imprisoned for violation of this same law and whose guilt may be less than mine. He could more closely approximate justice by pardoning them than by extending a pardon to me, a woman of wealth and influence." "It is true that I am the only woman to go to prison under the law," she added, "but I should receive no favors because of my sex."

The governor was not about to pardon the men of whom she spoke; but then, neither would he pardon her. In a statement he had distributed as a pamphlet by the thousands "in order that the people may know the truth regarding the case," the governor wrote that Whitney had a fair trial under a law that had been reviewed and retained by four successive legislative sessions. She herself had not asked for a pardon, he noted, and "those who have been convicted after fair trials, by juries sustained by decisions of courts, cannot expect to escape punishment of their crimes by appealing to me."

That seemed to be the end of the line. Appeals over, Whitney would have to go to prison. But as it turned out, there was yet another act to the Whitney drama.

CHAPTER FIVE

Thinking "Through" Free Speech

A number of people were central to the next developments in the *Whitney* case and to the evolution of American speech law. Justice Holmes was among them; so were lower federal court judge Learned Hand, Harvard Law School professor Zechariah Chafee, Communist Party leader Benjamin Gitlow, and a number of civil liberties lawyers. Perhaps the most important players, however, were Justice Brandeis and a former social worker named Roger Baldwin.

Louis Dembitz Brandeis's first conscious memory was of his mother taking food to the Union soldiers camped outside the family home in Louisville, Kentucky. His parents, who immigrated to the United States from Prague only a few years before his birth in 1856, supported the abolition of slavery. They also believed, fervently, in democracy, and in what they saw as the responsibility of citizens to participate actively in public life. Brandeis's favorite uncle was an attorney and public activist, and Brandeis decided to follow him into the law.

Brandeis graduated from Harvard Law School in 1878, with the highest grades ever earned at that institution, and soon opened a Boston law office with fellow graduate Samuel Warren. The firm prospered, and within a few years Brandeis felt sufficiently secure financially to devote increasing amounts of his time to public causes. Over the next decades he virtually created the position of the attorney who accepts public-interest cases without fee. At the same time, he led what was at least an equally active career outside the courtroom as an advocate in the political sphere. There he fought the trusts that were coming to control large portions of American economic life, advocated conservation of natural resources, mediated a 1912 strike of New York City garment workers, devised fair utility and transportation rates for Boston, invented savings bank life insurance, and advised and campaigned for Woodrow Wilson when Wilson ran for president in 1912.

Brandeis's father was a small businessman, so it is not surprising that Brandeis began his legal practice both convinced of the value of unfettered capitalism and suspicious of the developing labor movement. In 1902, however, a client who owned a shoe factory asked for his help. The business had fallen upon hard times and the workers were refusing to accept a temporary wage cut, in spite of what had been their unusually high wages. Visiting the plant and talking to the workers and to a union official who was helping them, Brandeis discovered that the employees were indeed paid well when they worked but that their work was seasonal and that there were many days when no work was to be had. He soon created a plan whereby the work could be spread out evenly over the year, satisfying both the client and the workers.

Impressed by the union men at the shoe factory, Brandeis was impelled to think about the position of labor in the United States. He had already heard pro-labor sentiments from some of the reformers whom he had met in the course of his public activism. Within a few years he joined the American Association for Labor Legislation, which he described as "designed to study labor problems and to agitate for favorable laws for workingmen." He called for recognition of the right of workers to unionize and advocated creation of a federal Department of Labor. He would eventually become a champion of unions and what he called "industrial democracy." "Industrial liberty must attend political liberty," he declared, and that meant putting labor on an equal footing with capital. "Unions and collective bargaining are essential to industrial liberty and social justice," he wrote to Ray Stannard Baker at the time of the textile strike in Lawrence, Massachusetts. While he held no brief for the I.W.W., sharing the popular view of it as overly radical and confrontational in its tactics, he recognized the gains it made for workers. When the Lawrence strike ended, he told another acquaintance that the strike had resulted in "very great immediate gains for the workers, and it is certainly a marvelous achievement for the I.W.W. men." Eventually, the man who had been skeptical of unions went so far as to assert that workers should be entitled to share in the profits of the businesses that benefited from their labor.

He had changed his mind about woman suffrage as well. "Have had a public career of late," he wrote to his brother in 1884. "Spoke against 'Woman Suffrage' before the [Massachusetts] Legislative Com[mit]tee yesterday." By 1911, however, he was presiding over a meeting of the Boston Equal Suffrage Association at which Jane Addams was the main speaker. He then went on to campaign for woman suffrage alongside his daughter Susan. "From having been of the opinion that we would advance best by leaving voting to men," he said in 1912, admitting to his initial conservatism, "I became convinced that we needed all the forces of the community to bring about this advance." It was women like Addams, with whom he had worked in reform movements, who had shown him that women could and should be as involved in the political process as men. He was persuaded "not only that women should have the ballot, but that society demands that they exercise the right."

Brandeis, in short, changed his mind when his experiences seemed to warrant it. As he had in the shoe factory dispute, he emphasized facts rather than theory as the basis for his beliefs. In 1908, he represented the National Consumers' League when an Oregon law establishing a maximum of ten hours' work a day for women employed in manufacturing, mechanical establishments, and laundries was challenged. He asked the League to provide him with statistics about the effects of long working hours on women. The League's effort was spearheaded by Brandeis's sister-in-law Josephine Goldmark, and when she presented him with reams of facts, he turned American constitutional litigation strategy on its head. He put the material into 110 pages designed to show an anti-labor Supreme Court that it was reasonable for Oregon, which shared the responsibility of all American states to provide for the health, safety, and welfare of its citizens, to limit women's paid working hours to a mere ten each day. Then he added only two pages of legal argumentation.

That was revolutionary. Supreme Court briefs of the time normally resembled Talmudic or Jesuitical treatises about the meaning of legal precedents; they did not instruct the justices on what was happening in the dynamic world of American society. Brandeis jettisoned over 100 years of American legal tradition and told the Court that law had to be based on the new realities of work in the industrial age.

In doing so, he was reflecting the thinking of one of the Supreme Court justices and a small number of other legal scholars. In 1881, years before Oliver Wendell Holmes was appointed to the Court, Holmes had helped create an approach to law that would come to be called sociological jurisprudence. "The life of the law has not been logic; it has been experience," he wrote in *The Common Law.* "The law embodies the story of a nation's development through many centuries, and it cannot be dealt with as if it contained only the axioms and corollaries of a book of mathematics." The idea that law had to change along with societal realities was still relatively new and not yet much in favor with many of the men on the Court.

Now, however, Brandeis told them that one of the new realities was that the excessive number of hours worked by women in industry endangered their well-being as well as that of their families. In a departure from the norm, the Supreme Court mentioned his brief in its decision, and upheld the Oregon law (*Muller v. Oregon*). What would become known as the fact-filled "Brandeis brief," which embodies the sociological jurisprudence approach, became a staple of American law. It was later employed, for example, in *Brown v. Board of Education* (1954), when Thurgood Marshall presented the Court with facts that demonstrated the negative effects of segregated schools on African American children, and in the cases that Ruth Bader Ginsburg took to the Court in the 1970s detailing the effects of gender discrimination on men and women. Brandeis would eventually unite his emphasis on facts with some serious reconsideration of his thinking about free speech, and that too would have a lasting effect on American jurisprudence.

Speech was particularly important to Brandeis during his career as a lawyer-activist. He believed absolutely in the power of ideas to persuade, although he would have called it education rather than persuasion. He was insistent that education was a lifelong process and that citizens of a democracy had to keep educating themselves in order to fulfill their civic responsibility. He told the Civic Federation of New England in 1906 that citizens had to be educated because they were the "rulers" of a democracy. "The citizen should be able to comprehend . . . the many great and difficult problems of industry, commerce and finance" he said, because they affect public policy decisions. He regularly turned to Progressive outlets such as *Collier's Magazine, Harper's Weekly,* and *La Follette's Weekly* as tools with which to educate the public, writing for them himself and urging that they publish their own articles about matters he thought should be of public concern. During one of his fights on behalf of the public, Brandeis called the press "our real Chorus"—a reference to the group in classical Greek plays that explained and commented upon the action taking place on stage. In 1901, Brandeis wrote to Edward Filene, publicity head of the Public Franchise League that had been formed in 1897 to prevent private control of street transportation: "Have editorials and similar notices in various papers, particularly the Springfield Republican, the Worcester Spay, and the Pittsfield papers. . . . Have personal letters written to members from the Metropolitan District . . . and have these persons ask for seats in the House during the debate. . . . Get as many letters into the Boston papers as you can." When he was fighting to have Massachusetts adopt the nation's first system of savings bank life insurance, he wrote to his brother about speaking about the issue to the Central Labor Union, the Unitarian Club, the Amalgamated Sheet Metal Workers, the Industrial League, and a Unitarian church. A few weeks after that he reported that he had spoken at two meetings the night before and had six more lectures coming up. Brandeis's letters from his pre-Court career are filled with the word "speech": reports of speeches he delivered before state legislatures and commissions, the U.S. Congress, and a host of federal agencies; speeches while he was campaigning for Woodrow Wilson; speeches to unions, businessmen's clubs, good government associations, schools, and religious groups. Convinced that reasonable people would ultimately come to accept the truth as he saw it, he was unfazed when faced with well-meaning dissent. "Differences in opinions are not only natural but desirable where the question is difficult; for only through such differences do we secure that light and fuller understanding which are necessary to a wise decision," he declared—a lesson gained from his public activism and, presumably, from his recognition that his own ideas had changed as that activism brought him into contact with people of many opinions. Brandeis's experience with public speech and its power to persuade would have a direct effect on his stance in Anita Whitney's case.

So would his understanding that taking unpopular stands required courage, which he believed to be one of the traits of democratic citizenship. Far from stifling speech, the government had an obligation to instill in its citizens what legal scholar Vincent Blasi has called "the ideal of civic courage": of participating in public discussion even when one's views may not be welcomed. Brandeis had seen that kind of personal courage writ large as civic courage in the adults in his abolitionist family, whose abhorrence of slavery made them highly unpopular with their Kentucky neighbors. He demonstrated it himself in the years before he was named to the Supreme Court. During his student days at Harvard and his early years as a practicing attorney, he was "taken up" by the elite Boston Brahmins, invited to their homes and their soirées. His experiences as a lawyer, however, convinced him that many of the ideas embraced by the welcoming Brahmins were wrong. He began to oppose their deeply held beliefs about the preponderant power employers should enjoy and their view of state legislatures as properly being little more than the instruments of the propertied classes. His popularity with many of his Brahmin acquaintances quickly disintegrated, but he was certain that as a citizen he had an obligation to speak for what was right. In his life, in making opponents of the rich and powerful, Brandeis had demonstrated his own civic courage. He equated it with freedom, believing that the willingness to face the vicissitudes of public life was a prerequisite of liberty. And involvement in public life required the freedom to speak.

Woodrow Wilson named Brandeis to the U.S. Supreme Court in 1916. Three years later, the relatively new justice voted with the majority to uphold the Espionage Act convictions of Charles Schenck, Jacob Frohwerk, and Eugene Victor Debs. In 1920, one year after that, Roger Baldwin became one of the organizers of the American Civil Liberties Union.

There is no record of Anita Whitney ever meeting Roger Baldwin, the co-founder and first executive director of the American Civil Liberties Union. The two activists came from remarkably similar backgrounds, however, and both Baldwin and the organization he played a leading role in creating would become crucial to Whitney's case. The odyssey of the California communist and the East Coast pacifist from their backgrounds in politically conservative families to the life of far more radical activists was, in a way, reflective of the ideological journey made by many politically involved citizens during the late nineteenth and early twentieth centuries. The sympathy of substantial numbers of Progressives with the labor movement led to their recognition that peaceful change in the economic and political systems was in part dependent on free speech.

Like Whitney, Baldwin could trace his ancestry to Pilgrims who arrived on the Mayflower. His father was the owner of a number of manufacturing companies and the family, like Whitney's, was comfortably well off. Roger Baldwin, born in 1884, grew up in a large house in Wellesley, Massachusetts. He and his family were living there when Whitney, seventeen years older than he, was studying at nearby Wellesley College. He spent his college years at Harvard, the institution Whitney's ancestors had helped found. After college he too went off for a tour of Europe.

Baldwin returned not sure of what he wanted to do with his life, thinking vaguely that he might enter his father's world of business. He turned for advice to Louis Dembitz Brandeis, then his father's lawyer, who advised him strongly to devote himself to public service. Baldwin took the advice and went off to St. Louis, where his life again tracked Whitney's. He became a social worker, as Whitney did; in his case, as director of a settlement house. His life paralleled hers once more when, in 1907, he was appointed as the chief probation officer of the St. Louis juvenile court and then became the unpaid secretary of the National Probation Officers Association. He, too, encountered Wobblies and was thoroughly impressed by them; so much so that Baldwin set up a lodging house in St. Louis with free food for the impoverished Wobblies who were spending their unemployed winters in the city. He told a biographer that he felt back then that he had accomplished nothing when compared to the I.W.W. organizers who risked their lives in western mining towns. According to an FBI report, Baldwin became a member of the Wobblies. In 1917 Baldwin moved to New York to donate his services to the American Union Against Militarism, the organization of which Whitney was a member. Like Whitney, Baldwin was radicalized both by direct experiences of others' poverty and by speakers excoriating it. "The more I saw of poverty and distress," he would say about his years in St. Louis, "the more I became convinced that social work alone was not enough." What had been his fairly apolitical ideas in college were challenged not only by his experiences as a social worker but by speeches by activists such as Emma Goldman, the anarchist and labor rights activist. Once the United States entered World War I in 1917, Baldwin organized a unit within AUAM in support of conscientious objectors, of whom he was one. He and Crystal Eastman, the AUAM executive secretary, gradually spun the unit off into a National Civil Liberties Bureau (NCLB) that focused on Wobblies and others who were jailed because of their speech. By then Baldwin was a staunch defender of both the labor movement and those who spoke out against the war. "The cause we now serve is labor," he declared, and all those who stood for the principle of freedom of expression.

There was some precedent for an organization devoted to the protection of speech. In 1873 Congress passed the anti-obscenity Comstock Act, which authorized the postal system to exclude "obscene" material from the mails. "Obscene" was not defined, and the Act was used to censor both sexually explicit and anarchist publications. Then, in 1901, President William McKinley was assassinated by an anarchist. Some states responded by enacting legislation designed to repress political speech. Others used laws such as those criminalizing incitement to riot as a way of punishing unpopular opinions. Legal historian David Rabban has shown that the laws prompted a number of left-wing activists to organize a Free Speech League, which held that free speech was crucial to individual autonomy and that the First Amendment protected both political and nonpolitical speech. The organization had close ties to the Wobblies, supporting them in their free speech fights, and helping to defend dissenters during World War I. Its key participants gradually moved away from the Free Speech League, and although it initially cooperated with the NCLB to some extent, the organization was effectively out of existence by the late 1920s.

The NCLB's defense of Wobblies being prosecuted under the Espionage Act soon earned the wrath of the Wilson administration. To explain its activities, the NCLB printed a 1918 pamphlet titled *The Truth About the I.W.W.*, arguing that the I.W.W. was a legitimate labor union that had not obstructed the war effort and was entitled to free speech. It published a variety of other pamphlets as well, including one on *Freedom of Speech and of the Press*. The Justice Department reacted to the NCLB's offerings by raiding its offices and seizing its files, and the Post Office put a dozen of the pamphlets on a list of publications banned from the mails. An NCLB attorney named Walter Nelles, about whom more later, persuaded a federal court to overturn the ban. The NCLB's landlord was not as forgiving. He told the organization it was no longer welcome and sent it on a difficult search for a new office.

On January 20, 1920, Eastman, Baldwin, and some of their colleagues officially reorganized the NCLB and spun it off as the independent American Civil Liberties Union (ACLU). Its first Statement of Purpose declared, "We stand on the general principle that all thought on matters of public concern should be freely expressed without interference. Orderly social progress is promoted by unrestricted freedom of opinion. The punishment of mere opinion, without overt acts, is never in the interest of orderly progress." The new ACLU retained the former NCLB's close ties to labor and began trying to obtain pardons for people convicted under the Espionage Act. For its efforts, it was attacked by, among others, United Mine Workers leader John L. Lewis, who called it "communistic," as well as the National Civic Federation, which described free speech as a "nuisance."

As part of its campaign to defend speech, the ACLU went to the Supreme Court in 1922 on behalf of a revolutionary socialist named Benjamin Gitlow—and later on behalf of Anita Whitney. It would face a court that was still upholding Espionage Act convictions but that was no longer unanimous in doing so.

In June 1919, just three months after the Supreme Court handed down its decisions in the *Schenck*, *Frohwerk*, and *Debs* cases discussed in chapter 2, the *Harvard Law Review* published an article entitled "Freedom of Speech in War Time" by the law school's Zechariah Chafee Jr. In it, Professor Chafee managed to eviscerate the clear and present danger test as it had been interpreted in those decisions, even while praising and revising it. The First Amendment's free speech clause, he wrote, "is a declaration of national policy in favor of public discussion of all public questions," and there was a good reason for it: "One of the most important purposes of society and government is the discovery and spread of truth on subjects of general concern. This is possible only through absolutely unlimited discussion." The mistake the Court made in upholding convictions such as Debs's under the Espionage Act, Chafee said, was that it did not utilize the clear and present danger test. He believed the facts in that case showed that Debs's speech created no clear and present danger. "The First Amendment forbids the punishment of words merely for their injurious tendencies," he argued, and so speech such as Debs's, which did not lead directly to an unlawful act, should not be punished.

Justices Holmes and Brandeis each read and were impressed by Chafee's article, and Brandeis cited it in a 1920 opinion. For Holmes, it tied in with an exchange of letters he was having with Judge Learned Hand, a federal lower court jurist.

There are three levels of courts in the federal judicial system: the district, or trial level courts; the circuit courts of appeals that cover multiple states; and the Supreme Court. Judge Hand sat on the district court for the Southern District of New York (he would later be appointed to the Court of Appeals for the Second Circuit, which hears cases from New York, Connecticut, and Vermont). As a district court judge, he presided over the 1917 case of *Masses Publishing Co. v. Patten* when Postmaster General Burleson used the Espionage Act to exclude an issue of the monthly left-wing journal *The Masses* from the mails. *The Masses* sought an injunction, prohibiting the postmaster from banning the magazine, and Hand granted it.

The issue of *The Masses* to which the postmaster objected contained antiwar and antidraft articles and cartoons, one of which depicted Uncle Sam in uniform, "all ready to fight for liberty," wearing handcuffs labeled "censorship" and a ball and chain dubbed "conscription." Looking at the word "cause" in the Espionage Act ("whoever, when the United States is at war . . . shall wilfully *cause* or attempt to cause insubordination, disloyalty, mutiny, refusal of duty, in the military or naval forces of the United States"), Hand held that reading it as broadly as the postmaster had done would lead to "the suppression of all hostile criticism, and of all opinion except what encouraged and supported the existing policies"—or, in other words, it would stifle dissent and public discussion of government policies. That in turn "would contradict the normal assumption of democratic government" that dissenting opinions should be allowed. Hand thought that Congress could not possibly have meant to do that when it passed the Act. Anticipating the position that Brandeis would arrive at ten years later in the *Whitney* case, Hand said that the government could punish "direct incitement to violent resistance" but not "political agitation," which was a "safeguard of free government." If a speaker "stops short of urging upon others that it is their duty or their interest to resist the law," then the speech must be allowed.

Hand's view of the Act, as we have seen, ran counter to the interpretation that Holmes and the Supreme Court would give it in the 1919 *Schenck, Frohwerk,* and *Debs* decisions. His ruling was in fact overturned by the Court of Appeals within a few months. Then, in June 1918, Holmes and Hand happened to meet on a train going from New York to Boston and began a conversation about the meaning of the free speech clause that they would continue by mail. Hand's biographer credits the correspondence with changing Holmes's attitude toward speech, although it seems clear that there were other forces at work as well. One of them was other members of the nation's legal elite, for by late 1919 some of them were attacking the Court's limitations on speech. In addition to Chafee's work, there was a veritable drumbeat of negative articles in Progressive magazines such as the *New Republic* and the *Nation.* Highly regarded University of Chicago law professor Ernst Freund wrote an article in the *New Republic* chastising Holmes and his speech decisions. Holmes was so taken aback by it that he commented on it in a letter to another frequent correspondent and drafted another letter—which he did not send—to the editor of the *New Republic,* defending himself.

While Holmes was being challenged to revise his ideas about speech, Brandeis was doing some rethinking of his own. The outcome would have a direct effect on Anita Whitney.

"I have never been quite happy about my concurrence" in the *Schenck* case, Brandeis told his friend Felix Frankfurter, then still a Harvard Law School professor, in 1924. When the case was decided, "I had not then thought the issues of freedom of speech out—I thought at the subject, not through it." He added that he considered the right to speech absolutely fundamental, along with the rights to education, to locomotion, and to choose one's profession.

His changed thinking, and that of Holmes, had become apparent even before Anita Whitney was put on trial. In late 1919, the Court handed down its opinion in the case of *Abrams v. United States.* There,

Holmes and Brandeis dissented for the first time from the Court's upholding of a conviction under the Espionage Act.

Jacob Abrams and four socialist and anarchist colleagues, all immigrants from Russia, had published English and Yiddish leaflets protesting what they described as capitalist-inspired American efforts to destroy the Russian Revolution. The leaflets criticized President Wilson, asserted that capitalism was the enemy of workers, and called for a general strike. Dissemination of the leaflets was extremely limited. As the Supreme Court acknowledged, the group "distributed" them primarily by having them tossed off a New York City rooftop. A store owner and three workmen who happened to pick them up took copies to the local police station. While it is difficult to see what seditious effect the leaflets might have had, Justice John H. Clarke and six other justices cited *Schenck* and *Frohwerk* in voting to uphold the group's convictions for interfering with the war effort.

Justice Holmes wrote a dissent for himself and Brandeis. Insisting both that "the principle of the right to free speech is always the same" and that the power to punish speech "is greater in time of war than in time of peace," Holmes interpreted the pamphlets as designed "to help Russia and stop American intervention there against the popular government—not to impede the United States in the war that it was carrying on." In addition, "nobody can suppose that the surreptitious publishing of a silly leaflet by an unknown man . . . would present any immediate danger that its opinions would hinder the success of the government arms or have any appreciable tendency to do so." There was, in short, no clear and present danger of damaging the war effort.

What was more important than Holmes's disagreement with the conviction, however, was the prose he penned about free speech. He rejected the idea that the government could always be trusted to find truth. "Persecution for the expression of opinions seems to me perfectly logical," he wrote. "If you have no doubt of your premises . . . you naturally express your wishes in law, and sweep away all opposition." But "truths" frequently change, and "when men have realized that time has upset many fighting faiths, they may come to believe even more than they believe the very foundations of their own conduct that the ultimate good desired is better reached by free trade in ideas—that the best truth is the power of the thought to get itself accepted in the competition of the market." If the nation was to find the policies that best suited it at any given moment, it had to allow the expression of all opinions "unless they so imminently threaten immediate interference with the lawful and pressing purposes of the law that an immediate check is required to save the country." That approach held dangers but, Holmes added, "That . . . is the theory of our Constitution. It is an experiment, as all life is an experiment."

Holmes nonetheless insisted that *Schenck, Debs,* and *Frohwerk* "were rightly decided." At the same time, however, he sent friends a series of letters privately expressing his dismay at having been assigned to write the opinions for the Court in the early Espionage Act cases, criticizing the prosecution of Debs, commenting that the lower federal judges presiding over Espionage Act prosecutions had been "hysterical about the war," and adding that many of those convicted—Debs among them—should be pardoned. Basically, Holmes thought that the law had been followed in the 1919 cases but that the Justice Department and the lower court judges should have exercised better judgment before prosecution or sentencing. He was not ready to call the decisions a mistake, but he was beginning to question the basis for them. Holmes did not say so but, in *Abrams,* he was finally turning "clear and present danger" into a more speech-permissive criterion than the "bad tendency" test. He apparently was still feeling his way through the difficult issues about the boundaries of free speech. So, by his own admission, was Justice Brandeis, who wrote dissents for himself and Holmes in *Schaefer v. United States* and *Pierce v. United States.*

Schaefer was the first Espionage Act case decided by the Court after *Abrams.* Peter Schaefer and four colleagues had been convicted for printing misleading articles about the war in the *Philadelphia Tageblatt* and the *Philadelphia Sonntagsblatt,* two German-language newspapers. The articles were contemptuous of the American war effort and suggested that the war was the doing of President Wilson, acting to serve England rather than the United States. Section three of the Espionage Act criminalizes "false reports or false statements" that are designed to "cause or attempt to cause insubordination, disloyalty, mutiny, refusal of duty" in the armed forces or obstruction in recruitment. Many of the two newspapers' articles were taken from other publications but not reprinted precisely as they appeared in those publications, and so the government accused the men in part of circulating "false" reports designed to hurt the war effort. Justice Joseph McKenna, writing in March 1920 for the Court's majority, lauded the convictions and took the occasion to lash out at anyone fighting a conviction under the Act. He cited *Schenck, Frohwerk, Debs,* and *Abrams* as sufficient refutation of its alleged unconstitutionality.

Brandeis reacted differently. It was "not until I came to write the Pierce and Schaefer cases," he told Frankfurter in their 1924 conversation, that he understood the issue of freedom of speech. Referring to then commerce secretary Herbert Hoover's belief that "criticism should end at [the] water's shore," meaning that there should be no disagreement with the government's foreign policy, he commented, "I felt just the opposite—wrote those long dissents in [the] Schaefer and Pierce cases to put on permanent record what we were not allowed to say." Rather than putting on record what one was not allowed to say, however, the dissents addressed what one should have been permitted to say, and that seemed to be virtually anything that would be permitted in peacetime.

Brandeis began his dissent in *Schaefer* by paying homage to the clear and present danger test. "This is a rule of reason," he declared, and "can be applied correctly only by the exercise of good judgment." That judgment, dependent on the content of the speech, "cannot be properly determined by culling here and there a sentence and presenting it separated from the context." (This was a clear slap at McKenna, who had done precisely that in his opinion.) The man of facts then included in his opinion four of the fifteen suspect publications so that people could see for themselves the context to which he referred.

Brandeis had grown up speaking German as well as English, and here his knowledge of German came into play. One charge in the government's indictment of the men was that a sentence had been added to a dispatch copied from a German newspaper, and so what purported to be the dispatch was "false." In fact, Brandeis said, that sentence followed the dispatch in the *Tageblatt* and was not presented as part of the dispatch itself. The government's translator made a mistake and included the sentence as part of the dispatch. "Evidently," Brandeis noted with no discernible hint of levity, "both the jury and the trial judge failed to examine the German original." What was more to the point, however, was that the articles were clearly "impotent to produce the evil against which the statute aimed." Since reasonable people could see that the articles would have no effect on the war effort, the jury that found the men guilty "must have supposed it to be within their province to condemn men, not merely for disloyal acts, but for a disloyal heart."

Brandeis added that suppression of such publications "subjects to new perils the constitutional liberty of the press." Then, citing Chafee and taking a page from the Harvard scholar's deliberate misreading of *Schenck*—presumably neither man wished to offend the elderly Holmes, whom they liked and admired—Brandeis added, "The constitutional right of free speech has been declared to be the same in peace and in war." That was of course not at all what Holmes declared in *Schenck*. It was, however, the altered position that Holmes took in *Abrams*, and so Brandeis, warning that limitations on speech during war could become limitations on speech in peacetime, implicitly went on with what would be the continuing reinterpretation of the clear and present danger test. The mere fact of war had been used in *Schenck* to make speech illegal. Brandeis was moving away from the idea that war alone was a justification for limiting speech, and Holmes was coming along with him.

A week later the Supreme Court announced its ruling in *Pierce v. United States*, the second Espionage Act case that led Brandeis to rethink his approach. It arose when four Albany, New York, socialists were convicted under the Act for circulating a pamphlet charging that the war had been started by capitalists to serve their own ends. Entitled *The Price We Pay*, the pamphlet also included language such as:

Conscription is upon us; the draft law is a fact!

Into your homes the recruiting officers are coming. They will take your sons of military age and impress them into the army;

Stand them up in long rows, break them into squads and platoons, teach them to deploy and wheel;

Guns will be put into their hands; they will be taught not to think, only to obey without questioning.

Then they will be shipped thru the submarine zone by the hundreds of thousands to the bloody quagmire of Europe.

Into that seething, heaving swamp of torn flesh and floating entrails they will be plunged, in regiments, divisions and armies, screaming as they go.

"These expressions," Justice Mahlon Pitney stated in his majority opinion for the Court, "were interspersed with suggestions that the war was the result of the rejection of Socialism, and that Socialism was the 'salvation of the human race.'" While some of the pamphlets had been coupled with a leaflet urging readers to join the Socialist Party, he said, the jury was well within its rights in disbelieving the defendants' statements at trial that they meant only to gain converts for the Socialist Party rather than to interfere with the conduct of the war.

Brandeis disagreed. He noted for himself and Holmes with what seemed to be a combination of amusement and dismay that in response to the "the recruiting officers are coming" language, the government had actually put a major with twenty-eight years' experience in the regular army on the stand to testify that gangs of recruiters did not break into American homes to seize potential soldiers. Including the entire pamphlet in his opinion, Brandeis asserted that "the cause of a war—as of most human action—is not single. War is ordinarily the result of many co-operating causes. . . . Historians rarely agree in their judgment as to what was the determining factor," and even the members of Congress who voted for a declaration of war disagreed with some of the reasons President Wilson gave them for American involvement. To treat the pamphlet's statements about the cause of the war as false, therefore, was to turn what was meant as expressions of opinion into false statements of fact. As for any clear and present danger of insubordination in the military or refusal to serve in it: "Certainly there was no clear and present danger that such would be the result. The leaflet was not even distributed among those in the military or the naval service." He warned that "the fundamental right of free men to strive for better conditions through new legislation and new institutions will not be preserved, if efforts to secure it by argument to fellow citizens may be construed as criminal incitement to disobey the existing law."

Brandeis continued to refine his approach to speech as he wrote a dissent in another wartime speech case that was appealed to the high court, this one involving a state rather than a federal statute. *Gilbert v. Minnesota* stemmed from a 1917 Minnesota statute that prohibited any interference with the military enlistment effort. Joseph Gilbert, an official of the Nonpartisan League, was convicted under it for telling a public meeting that the average person had nothing to say about whether the

United States should have become involved in World War I or whether a draft should have been imposed. Justice McKenna, again writing for the Court, declared that the law was merely designed "to preserve the peace of the state" in time of war, and he cited the Court's 1919 speech decisions. Brandeis, however, called the law "an act to prevent teaching that the abolition of war is possible" and noted that it, unlike the federal Espionage Act, was written to apply in peacetime as well as wartime. As he had warned in *Schaefer*, allowing the suppression of speech during wartime made it easier to suppress speech during peacetime.

Brandeis then added a statement that was ahead of the Court's view of speech but anticipated the way it would develop. The Court was still reading the First Amendment's speech clause as limiting only action by the federal government. Brandeis, however, rejected that idea, writing that the Minnesota law "affects rights, privileges, and immunities of one who is a citizen of the United States; and it deprives him of an important part of his liberty." The "rights, privileges, and immunities" phrase referred to is in the Fourteenth Amendment to the Constitution, which, as mentioned earlier, says in part, "No state shall make or enforce any law which shall abridge the privileges or immunities of citizens of the United States." Brandeis was arguing that free speech was one of the "rights" that belonged to all citizens and protected them from acts of *both* the federal and state governments.

He also began the process of explaining exactly why speech was necessary to a democratic society—a process that would culminate seven years later when the Court decided Anita Whitney's case. Exercise of the right to speak, Brandeis stated, was more than a privilege; it was a responsibility. Just as he had asserted that women had a responsibility to vote, once they had won the franchise, so he argued that all citizens in a democracy were obligated to participate in public affairs: "Full and free exercise of this right by the citizen is ordinarily also his duty; for its exercise is more important to the nation than it is to himself. . . . In frank expression of conflicting opinion lies the greatest promise of wisdom in governmental action; and in suppression lies ordinarily the greatest peril."

What exactly "the greatest peril" was remained unexplained, but Brandeis would spell it out when he wrote in *Whitney v. California*. In *Gilbert*, he began to explore the relationship between speech and democracy. "Wisdom in governmental action," to him, connoted governmental policies that benefited the greatest number of people. When he spoke in *Pierce* of "the fundamental right of free men to strive for better conditions through new legislation and new institutions," he had suggested a pragmatic reason for the free expression of ideas. Speech would lead to good government, which would in turn result in "better conditions."

There spoke the Progressive: the man who believed that government had to help citizens achieve the good life, which was attainable only through joint action. Brandeis was certain that the United States could be a place where justice for all was achieved. That could not happen, however, without the determined involvement of the citizenry and, as noted, he had written in *Gilbert* that each citizen had a duty to weigh in on government policies, for the citizen's participation in public affairs "is more important to the nation than it is to himself."

Before the Court got to *Whitney*, though, it would hear the ACLU-sponsored *Gitlow* case.

Benjamin Gitlow, a former member of the New York legislature, was convicted in 1920 for violating the state criminal anarchy law. The New York statute resembled California's criminal syndicalism law in criminalizing advocacy of any doctrine holding that "organized government should be overthrown . . . by any unlawful means." Like Anita Whitney, Gitlow was a member of the Left Wing of the Socialist Party. He was also the business manager of its official organ, *The Revolutionary Age*, which published the Left Wing's "Manifesto." Gitlow was in charge of paying for the Manifesto's printing and distribution.

Asserting that "the world is in crisis" and that capitalism was "in process of disintegration and collapse," the Manifesto lauded the Russian revolution and called for the destruction of the state through "the political mass strike." The objective was "the overthrow of the political organization upon which capitalistic exploitation depends, and the introduction of a new social system." That system was to be "Communist Socialism."

Gitlow was represented at his trial in 1920 by Clarence Darrow, with the assistance of the ACLU's Walter Nelles and Charles Recht. Gitlow did not actually meet Darrow until the night before the trial. The renowned lawyer was convinced that the case could not be won and indulged himself by delivering one of his famous diatribes, this one lauding revolution, as his closing statement to the jury. Nelles and Recht, however, focused on the speech issue. They argued that the New York law violated the Fourteenth Amendment's due process clause, which forbade states from depriving anyone of liberty without due process of law. Liberty, they told the court, included the right to free speech. They also asserted that even under the New York statute, language was criminal only if it was calculated to incite immediate illegal acts. The trial court, and the appeals courts after that, rejected those claims. Gitlow was sentenced to prison for five to ten years at hard labor.

Darrow bowed out of the case after the trial. When the verdict was appealed to the U.S. Supreme Court in 1922, Gitlow was represented by ACLU attorneys Nelles and Walter H. Pollak. It was the ACLU's first major appeal to the Supreme Court. Both men would be there again in Anita Whitney's case, so it is worth taking a moment to consider who they were and why they were involved in the litigation.

From its beginnings, the ACLU relied heavily on volunteer, or "cooperating," attorneys. It had little money for staff, and legal representation is costly. It turned in large part to lawyers who earned their money elsewhere and were willing to handle ACLU cases without pay. Pollak worked for high-powered New York City law firms from the moment he graduated from Harvard Law School. A well-regarded attorney, he was chosen during World War I to serve on the legal committee of the U.S. War Industries Board of the Council of National Defense, which was mandated to coordinate the nation's resources and industry in support of the war effort. He believed passionately in free speech and, in the 1920s, was one of the ACLU's busiest cooperating attorneys. In 1929 Pollak would be named to the staff of President Herbert Hoover's National Commission of Law Observance and Law Enforcement, better known as the Wickersham Commission. It studied criminal justice issues during the Prohibition era. Three years later he persuaded the U.S. Supreme Court to overturn the convictions of the Scottsboro boys, African American teenagers who had been tried by Alabama without adequate counsel and sentenced to death for the alleged rapes of two white women (*Powell v. Alabama*, 1932).

Walter Nelles, 42 years old at the time of *Gitlow*, also graduated from

Harvard Law School and practiced law in New York City. His practice focused on civil liberties, so it was not surprising that he became a lawyer first for the National Civil Liberties Bureau and then for the ACLU. In 1918 it was he who compiled a NCLB pamphlet that brought together and analyzed the early Espionage Act and state sedition cases. Roger Baldwin later commented that Nelles "had no private income and was obliged to accept a bare living wage to cover his expenses," which may be why Nelles returned to private practice in 1920. He retained his ACLU connection, however, as a cooperating attorney, and eventually became a highly regarded professor at Yale Law School.

The 35-year-old Pollak, who argued the *Gitlow* case before the Court, and Nelles, who worked with him on the briefs, believed that advocacy unaccompanied by any act was protected by the Constitution. "The citizen's liberty to take part in public affairs," they told the Court in an argument echoing what Justice Brandeis had written in *Gilbert* and foreshadowing what he would repeat in *Whitney*, is "in the interest of the whole community. . . . The citizen has a right to express, for the State may have an interest in hearing, any doctrine." Even if a belief was foolish or unpopular, the citizen had a constitutional right to articulate it as long as it was not connected to a crime.

Pollak and Nelles may have hoped for but probably did not expect victory, because the majority of the Court was still adhering to the "clear and present danger" doctrine as Justice Holmes had enunciated it in the *Schenck* case rather than as Holmes and Brandeis had reinterpreted it since then. They nonetheless had every reason to think that at least those two justices would be open to their argument.

They were right, but it was indeed only the two justices who would vote to overturn Gitlow's conviction. Justice Edward T. Sanford wrote the opinion for the seven-man majority upholding it. While acknowledging that "there was no evidence of any effect resulting from the publication and circulation of the Manifesto," Sanford declared that the test of criminality was not whether the speech urged immediate action. The New York law legitimately punished "advocacy of overthrow of organized government" because advocacy "impl[ies] urging to action." Sanford cited *Schenck*, his language suggesting that he and the other six justices gave it such a loose construction that their criterion resembled the bad tendency test.

The next part of Justice Sanford's opinion, however, represented a major change in the way the Court interpreted the First and Fourteenth Amendments. Pollak and Nelles had repeated the argument Nelles made during Gitlow's trial that the Fourteenth Amendment's due process clause incorporated the speech and press guarantees of the First Amendment—a position that the Court had never accepted. It did so now. "We may and do assume that freedom of speech and of the press—which are protected by the First Amendment from abridgment by Congress—are among the fundamental personal rights and liberties protected by the due process clause of the Fourteenth Amendment from impairment by the States," Sanford declared. The position that Justice Harlan had adopted way back in the 1907 case of *Patterson v. Colorado* (see chapter 2), when Harlan was a minority of one, was now the rule of law. Even Justice Holmes, who had written in *Patterson* that the First Amendment was not binding on the states, now agreed. *Gitlow* was the first time the Supreme Court held that one of the Bill of Rights' guarantees was binding on the states. Suddenly states, not just the federal government, were forbidden from abridging free speech, although Sanford qualified his statement with the "fundamental principle" that the right was not an absolute one. States could still punish speech that was "inimical to the public welfare, tending to corrupt public morals, incite to crime, or disturb the public peace." Gitlow's publication, containing "utterances endangering the foundations of organized government," fell into that category.

Holmes dissented once again, not from the incorporation of the speech and press clauses into the Fourteenth Amendment, but from the Court's endorsement of Gitlow's conviction. He insisted on behalf of himself and Brandeis that the clear and present danger test as enunciated in *Schenck* was still correct and should be applied in *Gitlow*. There was no attempt on Gitlow's part to overthrow the government, Holmes said, no incitement to immediate action, and therefore no clear and present danger. Then, in potent language that has also become a much-quoted classic of the law—Holmes was a master of quotable prose—he added:

It is said that this manifesto was more than a theory, that it was an incitement. Every idea is an incitement. It offers itself for belief and if believed it is acted on unless some other belief outweighs it or some failure of energy stifles the movement at its birth. The only difference between the expression of an opinion and an incitement in the narrower sense is the speaker's enthusiasm for the result. Eloquence may set fire to reason. But whatever may be thought of the redundant discourse before us it had no chance of starting a present conflagration. If in the long run the beliefs expressed in proletarian dictatorship are destined to be accepted by the dominant forces of the community, the only meaning of free speech is that they should be given their chance and have their way.

"My last performance during the term, on the last day," Holmes wrote to his friend Sir Frederick Pollak, "was a dissent . . . in favor of the rights of an anarchist (so-called) to talk drool in favor of the proletarian dictatorship."

When Holmes wrote that "every idea is an incitement," he presumably did not mean that every idea is an incitement to immediate action. Had that been his thinking, he logically would have voted with the majority. The "incitement" to which he referred was an invitation to thought and, possibly, later action. The dissents in *Abrams* and *Gitlow*, put together, amount to a statement that while "every idea is an incitement," the experiment in democratic governance enshrined in the Constitution demands that in the absence of immediate danger, all speech must be allowed. It would be left to Brandeis to explain that belief in detail when the Court handed down its decision in *Whitney*.

Gitlow had been out on bail during his appeals. Now he returned to prison, and the ACLU immediately petitioned New York Governor Al Smith to pardon him on the grounds that Gitlow's offense had involved only speech and that other people convicted under the act had served less prison time than he. Six months after the Court's ruling, Smith did pardon Gitlow. He issued a statement saying that while Gitlow was undeniably guilty, he had been in prison long enough; "many reputable citizens" had requested his release; and Holmes and Brandeis had indicated that Gitlow had not advocated anarchy—the crime of which he was accused—but merely "a new and radically different form of organized government."

A day later Gitlow walked out of Sing Sing with the usual state-provided suit of clothes and ten dollars. He met immediately with his supporters in the Workers' Party, which issued a statement lauding his release. The statement tied Gitlow's case to Whitney's: "The confirmation of the imprisonment of Charlotte Anita Whitney [referring to the Supreme Court's refusal to rule in her case] is again a demonstration that the capitalist class is pursuing a policy of persecution and oppression of the workers." Whitney had also seen a relationship between the two cases. In 1922, during that pre-Internet era, when Gitlow's appeal was still pending before the Supreme Court, she had written to attorney Neylan about it and had asked a friend to mail the relevant information to him.

Once Gitlow was pardoned, he returned to organizing and orating, exhorting laborers and others to unite and throw off the yoke of Wall Street. Three years later he ran on the Communist Party ticket for vice president of the United States. His major claim to historical fame, however, was his role as an unwitting contributor to the evolution of American speech law. And while the Supreme Court and the ACLU were now finished with Benjamin Gitlow's case, they were both about to play a part in Anita Whitney's.

CHAPTER SIX

"Public Discussion Is a Political Duty"

Walter Pollak and Walter Nelles had lost the *Gitlow* case, but the fact that the Supreme Court had accepted their argument that the right to free speech applied to the states gave them hope. They and Whitney's California lawyer John Neylan were already at work on an appeal to the Court to rehear the *Whitney* case, and the decision in *Gitlow* energized them. It was not, however, the only case the ACLU had pending in the high tribunal. The organization was also handling the appeal of Charles E. Ruthenberg. He, too, had been convicted of criminal syndicalism, and his case would have a direct effect on Whitney's.

Back in Chicago in 1919, when the Communist Labor Party was formed by former Socialists, others broke away from the Socialist Party to create the more radical Communist Party. Ruthenberg became its first national secretary, effectively the organization's leader. The 37-year-old Columbia Law School graduate and frequent Socialist Party candidate had already spent time in prison. Fervently antiwar, Ruthenberg had been convicted under the federal Conscription Act for making a speech that purportedly persuaded at least one draft-eligible young man not to register. The National Civil Liberties Bureau's Walter Nelles filed an *amicus* (friend of the court) brief on free speech grounds, but the U.S. Supreme Court upheld Ruthenberg's conviction, and he was imprisoned for ten months. Eugene Debs's antiwar speech in Canton, Ohio—the speech for which he was convicted under the Espionage Act—was reportedly given after he visited Ruthenberg in jail.

Once Ruthenberg was released, he maintained a nonstop schedule of speaking engagements across the country, which led to charges under various states' criminal syndicalism or criminal anarchy statutes. By 1919 the *Chicago Daily Tribune* was referring to Ruthenberg as the "most arrested Red" in the country, claiming that there were more than sixty indictments pending against him. In 1920 he was sentenced to prison in New York, under the same criminal statute that had been used against Benjamin Gitlow. He was released from Sing Sing in 1922. Shortly thereafter, he was arrested under Michigan's criminal syndicalism law for participating in a supposedly secret gathering that was designed to bring together the official Communist Party of America and various dissident factions. The meeting, Michigan charged, was an illegal assembly because the Communist Party was "formed to teach or advocate the doctrines of criminal syndicalism."

The young ACLU had already decided to mount a concerted attack on criminal syndicalism laws, and Roger Baldwin quickly offered Ruthenberg its services. The organization engaged attorney Frank P. Walsh to represent Ruthenberg and added Walter Nelles and a Michigan attorney to the legal team. Ruthenberg was found guilty in spite of their efforts, and in 1924 the conviction was upheld by the Michigan Supreme Court.

The attorneys then sought review by the U.S. Supreme Court, citing *Gitlow* and claiming that the Michigan law violated the speech and due process clauses of the First and Fourteenth Amendments. The Court heard oral argument in the case in 1926. A majority voted to uphold the conviction. Brandeis, who by then had thought "through" the subject of speech as he told Frankfurter he had not in 1919, began to draft a dissent for himself and Justice Holmes.

The "crime" of which Ruthenberg had been found guilty, Brandeis wrote, was that of voluntarily assembling with an organization that advocated criminal syndicalism. The right of assembly was intimately connected to the right to free speech, and so could be restricted only if "its exercise involves clear and present danger." The question was whether Ruthenberg's act of assembly did constitute such a danger, and who or what should make that assessment.

Brandeis made no secret of his distaste for the Communist Party and its ideology. He was dismayed by its goal of creation of a proletarian dictatorship and spoke of its "false assertions," "fallacious reasoning," and "foul doctrine." He recognized that the party taught that force would be necessary to achieve its purpose, and made clear that he could not condone that. Citing Learned Hand's opinion in the *Masses* case,

Brandeis acknowledged that "every denunciation of existing law tends in some measure to increase the probability that there will be some violation of it." But, he added, "even advocacy of violation, however reprehensible morally, is not a justification for denying free speech, where, as here, the advocacy falls short of incitement." The man of facts went on to declare that the party's use of force in 1922, when Ruthenberg's trial took place, was "a remote contingency. The Party had then less than six thousand members, scattered throughout the United States . . . all but five thousand were . . . of small means and unfamiliar with the English language. The aggregate of a year's expenditures for all its activities was $185,715." As a result, "the process of converting any substantial portion of the thirty million American workers to revolutionary views would necessarily be a slow one," leaving "ample time and opportunity" to counteract the party's teachings with "sound argument." Nothing in Ruthenberg's past suggested that he was likely to advocate immediate violence. "There is not even a suggestion that Ruthenberg had . . . committed, or attempted or conspired to commit, or had incited any other person to commit, any act of violence or terrorism." Bad speech could be countered with good speech, Brandeis asserted. There was in fact no imminent danger.

Brandeis rejected the notion that the legislature's enactment of a criminal syndicalism statute declaring advocacy to be a crime was enough to prove that such advocacy *should* be criminalized. Ruthenberg's jury should have been instructed "that there must be a clear and present danger of immediate violence to justify conviction," but that did not happen. In the absence of such a showing, the conviction could not be sustained.

Acknowledging Chafee's influence on his thinking, Brandeis cited the law professor twice in his opinion. He also quoted Thomas Jefferson's First Inaugural Address: "If there be any among us who wish to dissolve the union or change its republican form, let them stand undisturbed as monuments of the safety with which error of opinion may be tolerated where reason is left free to combat it." Brandeis wrote at length about the Founding Fathers' reasons for amending the Constitution to guarantee free speech and assembly, in order to encourage the exchange of ideas crucial to a democracy.

It looked for a moment as if that language would go unread, however.

The Court never issued a ruling in the Ruthenberg case. Ruthenberg died on March 2, 1927, after an appendicitis operation and before the decision could be handed down. That mooted the case; Brandeis's dissent, as well as the Court's holding, went unpublished. He would still be able to use his opinion, however, because the Court had accepted Whitney's lawyers' plea to hear *Whitney v. California* again. At the attorneys' request, the District Court of Appeal had issued a certificate stating that in deciding the case, the court had considered the question of whether the criminal syndicalism law and its application to Whitney were in violation of the Fourteenth Amendment. That meant the case as argued in the courts below involved interpretation of the U.S. Constitution, and so the Supreme Court had jurisdiction over it.

The Court heard oral argument in *Whitney* for a second time on March 18, 1926. After Ruthenberg's death almost a year later, Brandeis would tinker with the *Ruthenberg* language and turn it into his opinion in Anita Whitney's case.

Neylan and the ACLU lawyers were able to continue pursuing Whitney's case in part thanks to a young Boston philanthropist. In 1920, when his stockbroker father died, 21-year-old Charles Garland found himself with an inheritance of close to a million dollars. His initial reaction was to refuse it because, he said, he had not earned it, and it was the result of an unfair and exploitative economic system. At the urging of crusading author Upton Sinclair that he use the money for philanthropy, Garland held off his decision to turn the inheritance down. The following year Walter Nelles married Garland's mother. It is probable that Nelles was responsible for bringing Garland and Roger Baldwin together. Baldwin persuaded Garland to accept the inheritance and use it to establish a fund that would back progressive causes. The new fund they established was given the formal name of the American Fund for Public Service (AFPS) and was known less formally as the Garland Fund. Its board of directors included many people prominent in the ACLU, who served without pay alongside labor and minority group leaders. The group of advisors who reviewed applications to it was made up at various times of luminaries such as John Dewey, Jane Addams, Felix Frankfurter, and Walter Lippman. As the American stock market rose dramatically in the

1920s, the fund's value almost doubled in size, and it was soon award-
ing grants to the International Ladies' Garment Workers' Union, the
League for Industrial Democracy, the American Birth Control League,
the National Association for the Advancement of Colored People, and
other entities considered by the fund to "promote the well-being of
mankind throughout the world."

The ACLU was among the groups that benefited. The AFPS soon
created an emergency fund that was to be used largely for ACLU cases
and that was regularly drawn upon. By 1925 the ACLU was getting AFPS
money for both the *Whitney* appeal and a campaign to have the California criminal syndicalism law repealed. When the Supreme Court
refused to decide Whitney's case that year, a leader of the California
branch of the ACLU wrote that "there is tremendous feeling here over
her plight . . . the Whitney case now offers the big opportunity here for
action against the C.S. [criminal syndicalism] law and its victims." Whitney agreed. There were "over eighty I.W.W. boys . . . in San Quentin and
Folsom" as a result of criminal syndicalism convictions, she wrote to the
AFPS secretary. "I think public opinion must be changed and I cannot
see why the present time is not ripe." By 1925 the ACLU was using AFPS
grants on the repeal effort as well as to reimburse Whitney's lawyers for
stenographic services, phone bills, and printing expenses. The payments
to the attorneys would continue into 1927. Additional money for the case
came from Whitney, who was selling some of what remaining property
she had in order to contribute to it. Neylan was also trying to raise funds
for the litigation.

In late 1925 Neylan, Nelles, and Pollak presented the Supreme Court
with an eighty-four-page brief arguing that due process had been violated when Whitney was denied the specifics of the charges against
her; all discussion of the Chicago convention and the Wobblies should
have been excluded from evidence because there was no indication that
Whitney was involved with them; the Oakland convention did nothing
to incite criminal activity, and in any event Whitney could not be punished for the language of a resolution passed as a substitute for hers; and
the criminal syndicalism law was an unconstitutional prior restraint on
the rights of speech and assembly. The only thing that should have been
considered at her trial, they told the court, was the happenings at the
Oakland convention. Downplaying the importance of even that event,

they noted, "Defendant in attending had no purpose of helping to create an instrument of terrorism and it was not her purpose, nor, as far as she knew or could know, the purpose of the convention—if an inchoate organization of this character could be said to have anything so unified as a purpose—to do anything unlawful."

California replied that Whitney had voted for what it called the "radical" delegates to the Chicago convention, so she was implicitly responsible for whatever they did. The evidence introduced about the national CLP and the Wobblies was completely germane, the state argued, because it showed the "character" of the California CLP, which was in turn made clear by activities of the I.W.W. The state's brief included pages of verbatim quotes from the national CLP's platform and also repeated the point Harris had attempted to make at trial, that one of the resolutions at the convention had "recommended *forcing the release* of class war prisoners."

The majority of the justices sided with California. They were no more impressed by Pollak, Nelles, and Neylan's arguments in *Whitney* than they had been by the ACLU lawyers' reasoning in *Ruthenberg*. Justice Edward T. Sanford declared for himself and six of the other eight justices—everyone but Brandeis and Holmes—that the California syndicalism law was perfectly constitutional. "The essence of the offense denounced by the Act is the combining with others in an association for the accomplishment of the desired ends through the advocacy and use of criminal and unlawful methods. It partakes of the nature of a criminal conspiracy." Such "united and joint action," Sanford continued, "involves even greater danger to the public peace and security than the isolated utterances and acts of individuals," and the state had every right to outlaw it. The law was not vague, and so did not violate due process; it did not, as Whitney's attorneys had argued, violate the equal protection clause by singling out speech advocating changes in the political structure but not speech applauding the status quo.

As for the assertion that Whitney should not be held liable for a resolution that she had opposed at the convention, Sanford wrote, "This contention, while advanced in the form of a constitutional objection to the Act, is in effect nothing more than an effort to review the weight of the evidence for the purpose of showing that the defendant did not join and assist in organizing the Communist Labor Party of California with a knowledge of its unlawful character and purpose." The jury had reviewed the facts and found otherwise, Sanford said. The court would follow proper appellate procedure by declining to revisit the jury's findings. But just to make clear that the court agreed with the jury, Sanford continued, "And we may add that the argument entirely disregards the facts: that the defendant had previously taken out a membership card in the National Party, that the resolution which she supported did not advocate the use of the ballot to the exclusion of violent and unlawful means of bringing about the desired changes in industrial and political conditions; and that, after the constitution of the California Party had been adopted, and this resolution had been voted down and the National Program accepted, she not only remained in the convention, without protest, until its close, but subsequently manifested her acquiescence by attending as an alternate member of the State Executive Committee and continuing as a member of the Communist Labor Party."

Brandeis disagreed with every part of the majority's reasoning and made that clear in the opinion he drafted for himself and Justice Holmes.

It is odd to realize now that as of 1927, Americans took the right to free speech for granted, but no member of the Supreme Court— perhaps no one in a position of political power in the United States— had ever laid out a thorough explanation for why allowing it was a good thing. Judge Hand alluded to it in the *Masses* case discussed in the previous chapter, and Justice Holmes may have come close when he wrote in *Abrams v. United States* that "the ultimate good desired is better reached by free trade in ideas—that the best test of truth is the power of the thought to get itself accepted in the competition of the market." Exactly what that "ultimate good" was, however, remained unexplained. Truth, Holmes had suggested, was anything but eternal: what the majority of people—the denizens of the marketplace of ideas—believed at any given moment was defined as truth. "If in the long run the beliefs expressed in proletarian dictatorship are destined to be accepted by the dominant forces of the community, the only meaning of free speech is that they should be given their chance and have their way," Holmes had written in his *Gitlow* dissent. To him, free speech was the mechanism by which the "dominant forces of the community" would decide what laws they wanted. Whatever those "dominant forces" chose was acceptable. Life was a game that Holmes watched with a strong measure of cynicism. "If my fellow citizens want to go to Hell I will help them," he wrote to a friend. "It's my job."

Brandeis, on the other hand, believed that there were immutable truths, and one of them was the virtue of democracy. Democracy, as he saw it, would provide governmental policies that benefited the citizenry as a whole while enhancing the individual's ability to lead a good life. The justice, his colleague Alvin Johnson commented, was an "implacable democrat." One of his law clerks went further, suggesting that to Brandeis, "democracy is not a political program. It is a religion." The question was how to keep democracy safe and enable it to flourish.

Brandeis and Holmes seemed on paper to reach the same place where speech rights were concerned, but they got there by decidedly different routes. Like Holmes, Brandeis put his faith in the marketplace of ideas; unlike Holmes, he believed that the choices made in it mattered, and ultimately would be the correct ones. David Riesman, one of Brandeis's clerks, noted that while Brandeis was "skeptical of power and of human abilities," he also had "an extraordinary faith in the possibilities of human development," and he trusted the electorate to find truth. Perhaps the difference lay in the backgrounds of the two men. Holmes's experiences were largely confined to the world of the Boston Brahmin except for the traumatic service in the Civil War that helped turn him into a social Darwinist who believed in survival of the fittest. Brandeis, on the other hand, had experience of laborers whose education had been minimal but whose ideas seemed far more rational to him than did those of many Brahmins. His skepticism was reserved for the wealthy elite—precisely those people Holmes might have seen as the "fittest"—and for the assumption that any group of human beings in or outside the government always knew what was best for all.

Now, finally thinking "through" all the reasons that speech had to be free, Brandeis redefined the clear and present danger doctrine. "This Court has not yet fixed the standard by which to determine when a danger shall be deemed clear; how remote the danger may be and yet be deemed present, and what degree of evil shall be deemed sufficiently substantial to justify resort to abridgement of free speech and assembly as the means of protection," he wrote in *Whitney*. "To reach sound conclusions on these matters, we must bear in mind why a State is, ordinarily, denied the power to prohibit dissemination of social, economic and political doctrine which a vast majority of its citizens believes to be false and fraught with evil consequence." He then laid out a rationale for free speech in a democracy, and placed it firmly in the context of American history and ideology. Some of his paragraphs are lengthy, but they must be read as a piece if they are to be understood and if the persuasive power of his prose is to be appreciated. He began by summarizing his reading of the intentions of the Founding Fathers.

Those who won our independence believed that the final end of the State was to make men free to develop their faculties; and that in its government the deliberative forces should prevail over the arbitrary. They valued liberty both as an end and as a means. They believed liberty to be the secret of happiness and courage to be the secret of liberty. They believed that freedom to think as you will and to speak as you think are means indispensable to the discovery and spread of political truth; that without free speech and assembly discussion would be futile; that with them, discussion affords ordinarily adequate protection against the dissemination of noxious doctrine; that the greatest menace to freedom is an inert people; that public discussion is a political duty; and that this should be a fundamental principle of the American government.

That paragraph contains a number of ideas leading to the conclusion that speech is vital to a democracy. In writing that "those who won our independence believed that the final end of the State was to make men free to develop their faculties," Brandeis indicated that he viewed the goal of the American Revolution to have been creation of the circumstances under which individuals could fulfill themselves according to their abilities. Government was properly created by human beings to achieve goals unattainable without a State, among them the liberty necessary to develop individual talents. Liberty was "the secret of happiness." But the Framers, in Brandeis's interpretation, saw freedom as more than a goal. To them, liberty—which includes the right to free speech—was both "an end and . . . a means." They understood that finding "political truth"—that is, answers to the question of what would best serve society and the individuals in it—was dependent upon full discussion, itself in turn dependent on "free speech and assembly."

Brandeis had long steeped himself in ancient Greek history and was a great admirer of Athens in the fifth century BC. The highest praise he could bestow was to say of a person that "he reminded one of the Athenians." When Brandeis wrote that the Founding Fathers "believed liberty to be the secret of happiness and courage to be the secret of liberty," he was quoting directly from Pericles's "Funeral Oration"—an oration extolling democracy that the Athenian statesman delivered in the year 431 BC. Democracy took courage, Brandeis believed: the courage of the individual to express opinions that might not be popular and the courage of the society to allow such speech to be heard.

To Brandeis, speech was both something of a panacea and an obligation. When he wrote that "discussion affords ordinary adequate protection against the dissemination of noxious doctrine," he was asserting that incorrect ideas would soon be exposed as such if they were held up to public scrutiny. That did not mean that people could not be misled by wrong ideas: the Founding Fathers "recognized the risks to which human institutions are subject." They also knew, however, that democracy required "public discussion" rather than "an inert people."

James Madison wrote in number 51 of the Federalist Papers, "If men were angels, no government would be necessary. . . . If angels were to govern men, neither external nor internal controls on government would be necessary. In framing a government which is to be administered by men over men, the great difficulty lies in this: you must first enable the government to control the governed; and in the next place oblige it to control itself." Brandeis agreed. Like Madison, Brandeis saw the state as an inevitably imperfect instrument, not only because "arbitrary" forces will challenge "deliberative" forces and because institutions are run by fallible human beings, but because it is in the nature of humanity to generate and heed "evil counsels," at least temporarily. No government is to be entirely trusted, no matter who its administrators are, and every democratic government must be subjected to constant examination by the people.

At the same time, again reflecting his background as a Progressive, Brandeis insisted that a balance must be struck between two societal imperatives: the first, a government strong enough to protect citizens from overzealous majorities; the other, the kind of protection needed by citizens from that very government. The Founders, he continued, recognized the risks to which all human institutions are subject. But they knew that order cannot be secured merely through fear of punishment for its infraction; that it is hazardous to discourage thought, hope and imagination; that fear breeds repression; that repression breeds hate; that hate menaces stable government; that the path of safety lies in the opportunity to discuss freely supposed grievances and proposed remedies; and that the fitting remedy for evil counsels is good ones. Believing in the power of reason as applied through public discussion, they eschewed silence coerced by law—the argument of force in its worst form. Recognizing the occasional tyrannies of governing majorities, they amended the Constitution so that free speech and assembly should be guaranteed.

Brandeis was not naïve. He understood that ideas could be dangerous, and made it clear that he worried about precisely the kind of "noxious" ideas that Anita Whitney believed in. "Every denunciation of existing law tends in some measure to increase the probability that there will be a violation of it," he acknowledged, repeating the language he had first written in *Ruthenberg*. "Condonation of a breach enhances the probability. Expressions of approval add to the probability. Propagation of the criminal state of mind by teaching syndicalism increases it. Advocacy of law-breaking heightens it still further." And yet those risks did not negate the greater danger of government repression. When speech is repressed, what follows is the "hate" that "menaces stable government." Stability and lawfulness were crucial to a free society. The safest course was not to repress speech but to count on "the power of reason as applied through public discussion." People could be misled, but not permanently, and so Brandeis fashioned a standard that he was convinced would protect both speech and the security of the nation. Invoking another moment in early American history when, in the seventeenth century, the citizens of Salem, Massachusetts, killed women they believed to be witches, he wrote:

Fear of serious injury cannot alone justify suppression of free speech and assembly. Men feared witches and burnt women. It is the function of speech to free men from the bondage of irrational fears. To justify suppression of free speech there must be reasonable ground to fear that serious evil will result if free speech is practiced. There must be reasonable ground to believe that the danger apprehended is imminent . . . even advocacy of violation, however reprehensible morally, is not a justification for denying free speech where the advocacy falls short of incitement and there is nothing to indicate that the advocacy would be immediately acted on. The wide difference between advocacy and incitement, between preparation and attempt, between assembling and conspiracy, must be borne in mind. In order to support a finding of clear and present danger it must be shown either that immediate serious violence was to be expected or was advocated, or that the past conduct furnished reason to believe that such advocacy was then contemplated.

Fear that words *might* be persuasive is not sufficient reason to ban or punish them, Brandeis declared in that paragraph. The clear and present danger doctrine means that speech cannot be suppressed unless it is "reasonable" to believe that "serious" and "imminent" evil is about to occur. If this implies that most reasonable people, or all the members of a jury, must agree that specific speech will cause serious and imminent evil, an agreement that a governmental limitation on speech was "reasonable" will be extremely hard to reach—and that is entirely appropriate. Moreover, it is not enough for the danger to be "clear"; it must be "serious." Similarly, it has to be more than "present"; it has to be "imminent." Elaborating on the meaning of "imminent," and once again citing the beliefs of the Founding Fathers, Brandeis continued:

Those who won our independence by revolution were not cowards. They did not fear political change. They did not exalt order at the cost of liberty. To courageous, self-reliant men, with confidence in the power of free and fearless reasoning applied through the processes of popular government, no danger flowing from speech can be deemed clear and present, unless the incidence of the evil apprehended is so imminent that it may befall before there is opportunity for full discussion. If there be time to expose through discussion the falsehood and fallacies, to avert the evil by the processes of education, the remedy to be applied is more speech, not enforced silence.

"Education" in that paragraph did not mean schooling, but the kind of education that occurs when citizens talk with each other about public matters. As long as there was time for more reasonable voices to respond, speech, however noxious, could not be abridged or punished. Speech could not be suppressed unless there was imminent danger, and the danger had to be extreme. "The fact that speech is likely to result in some violence or in destruction of property is not enough to justify its suppression." The sole triggering element that would permit suppression of speech was "the probability of serious injury to the State," and that could occur only if there was an "emergency [that] does not permit reliance upon the slower conquest of error by truth." Speech that resulted in violence or destruction of property might be punished, but it could not be stopped. People could be silenced only if there was imminent "probability of serious injury to the State," because "among free men, the deterrents ordinarily to be applied to prevent crime are education and punishment for violations of the law, not abridgement of the rights of free speech and assembly." Brandeis trusted that truth ordinarily would conquer error; otherwise, democracy made no sense. Perhaps more importantly, he believed that the difficult job of engaging in debate and refuting error, unlike the comparatively easy method of suppressing it, would contribute to building democratic habits and character. The answer to bad speech was good speech, and lots of it.

Brandeis was following Chafee in his creation of a highly permissive standard for speech. The "boundary line of free speech," Chafee had written in the *Harvard Law Review* article that Brandeis found so compelling, was "fixed close to the point where words will give rise to unlawful acts. . . . And we can with certitude declare that the First Amendment forbids the punishment of words merely for their injurious tendencies. The history of the Amendment and the political function of free speech corroborate each other and make this conclusion plain."

Brandeis's approach to speech dovetailed nicely with his firm belief in capitalism regulated by the government. He viewed radical movements in the United States as a logical if lamentable reaction to the concentration of money and power in the hands of too few people and too big trusts. Convinced that competition among moderately sized businesses was one of the keys to an economy that would benefit all citizens, Brandeis had helped Woodrow Wilson hammer out a platform of controlling the trusts when Wilson first ran for president in 1912. The necessary reforms would not be achieved and radicalism would not be contained, Brandeis thought, if ideas that at first hearing might seem outrageous or subversive were stifled. In that sense, the economic as well as the political prosperity of the nation depended upon free speech.

Economic prosperity also required experimentation, and Brandeis wanted the Court to stay out of the way of such experiments. His reputation as one of the nation's outstanding justices rests in part on his embrace of judicial restraint and his insistence that, particularly in the economic sphere, governmental experimentation had to be given the benefit of the constitutional doubt. If a state government or the federal government chose to enact economic legislation in order to create what it believed would be a more just society, Brandeis would vote to permit it to do so, whether or not he agreed with the law. Justice Holmes had suggested that for the most part the elected branches of the government had the power to regulate the economy as they saw fit. Brandeis fleshed that idea out, arguing that the states in particular but the federal government as well had to be permitted to experiment with novel approaches to the economy and to the way they exercised their power generally.

As *Whitney* demonstrates, Brandeis did not believe that the same kind of deference to the legislature applied when the government acted in the area of speech. There, he argued, the Supreme Court had quite a different role than it did in litigation involving matters such as regulation of commerce. Misguided commercial policies might hurt the economy for a time, but they would not affect the democratic nature of the state, which would in fact be reinforced by permitting the people's representatives to try what they considered best. Legislative interference with speech, however, was interference with democracy itself. A law that stifled dissent and unpopular ideas not only hurt liberty; it also impeded the very process of experimentation and assessment of such experiments that enabled societies to progress. In *Whitney* and the cases leading up to it, Brandeis in effect signaled what would become the "preferred freedoms" doctrine articulated in 1938 by Justice Benjamin Cardozo and subsequently followed by the Supreme Court. "Preferred freedoms" holds that when the government regulates the civil liberties guaranteed to Americans by the Bill of Rights and later constitutional amendments, the courts will examine the action with skepticism, and it is up to the government to prove that the regulation is legitimate, necessary, and as least intrusive as it can be. The result is quite different from the assumption made by courts when the government acts in other areas of the law, where the burden is on anyone challenging the law to demonstrate that it is unreasonable.

All of that lay behind Brandeis's opinion in *Whitney*. It would become the defining justification for free speech in the United States, and was also an example of the way justices—and the public policies they affect—reflect their lives and the ideas current in society at any given moment. Most justices are particularly aware of ideas circulating among the legal elite.

Chafee qualifies as part of that group. Scholars today disagree about whether the Founding Fathers actually intended the speech clause to be as permissive as Brandeis claimed. In asserting his version of history and clothing himself in the mantle of the Framers, Brandeis was once again following Chafee. He paralleled Chafee as well in setting the dividing line between permissible and impermissible speech at incitement. "If the Supreme Court [clear and present danger] test is to mean anything more than a passing observation," Chafee had written, "it must be used to upset convictions for words when the trial judge did not insist that they must create 'a clear and present danger of overt acts.'"

Chafee, for his part, was following Judge Learned Hand's opinion in the *Masses* case discussed in chapter 5. "There is no finer judicial statement of the right of free speech" than that opinion, Chafee wrote in his *Harvard Law Review* article, and he dedicated his subsequent volume *Freedom of Speech* to Hand. "It was really your opinion in the *Masses* case that started me on my work" in the speech field, Chafee told Hand. "If one stops short of urging upon others that it is their duty or their interest to resist the law, it seems to me one should not be held to have attempted to cause its violation," Hand had said in that case, in effect anticipating Brandeis's emphasis on immediate incitement as the test. Brandeis cited both Hand's opinion and Chafee's volume in a footnote to his own opinion in *Whitney*.

In the eight years between the Supreme Court's decisions in *Schenck* and *Whitney*, Chafee, Hand, and Holmes all discussed with each other the limits that could or should not be placed on speech. Chafee had tea with Holmes in 1919, before Holmes wrote his dissent in *Abrams v. United*

States, and pressed the justice to liberalize his approach to speech. Chafee corresponded with Hand; Hand, with Holmes. Hand would have set the line at which speech could be punished at incitement to a crime; Chafee and Holmes preferred the more speech-restrictive clear and present danger test. All, though, agreed that the standard had to be far more permissive than the "bad tendency" test preferred by the majority of justices then on the Supreme Court.

Brandeis was an active participant in the exchange of ideas. Chafee sent part of his yet unpublished *Freedom of Speech* to Dean Acheson, his former student at Harvard and by then Brandeis's law clerk, while the Supreme Court was considering *Gilbert v. Minnesota*. Acheson passed it along to Brandeis. When the Court announced its decision in *Gilbert*, Brandeis wrote to Felix Frankfurter, "Tell me frankly whether you or Chaffee [*sic*] see any flaw in the reasoning in the dissent." He asked for Chafee's opinion again after the Court published its decision in *Milwaukee Social Democratic Publishing Company v. Burleson*, another Espionage Act case in which Brandeis dissented. "I have been re-reading Chafee's Freedom of Speech with ever growing admiration of his head, his heart and his character," Brandeis told Frankfurter in 1926, while the justice was working on his opinion in *Whitney*. Chafee, in turn, said he was influenced by Walter Nelles, whose collection and analysis of Espionage Act cases Chafee cited on the first page of his *Harvard Law Review* article. Brandeis corresponded with Hand, and the two men talked whenever Hand was in Washington. Once *Whitney* was handed down, Brandeis sent copies of it to Chafee and Hand.

In other words, the meaning of free speech had become a concern for a number of American legal thinkers, as exemplified by Holmes, Hand, and Chafee, as well as for the attorneys of the ACLU. Brandeis's *Whitney* opinion has to be understood in the light of that dialogue, and there were influences from outside the legal profession as well. By 1927 the country had moved beyond its postwar hysteria. In March 1919, accepting a recommendation from departing Attorney General Thomas Gregory, President Wilson released or reduced the sentences of 200 people convicted under the Espionage and Sedition Acts. (He declined, however, to release Eugene Debs, who remained in prison until he was pardoned by President Warren Harding in December 1921.) In 1921 Congress repealed the Sedition Act, although the Espionage Act was allowed to remain on the books. The last prisoners convicted under the Espionage Act were released in December 1923 by President Calvin Coolidge. By 1927 most of the Wobblies convicted under various criminal syndicalism laws had been pardoned.

Brandeis, then, was not entirely alone in thinking "through" the reasons for freedom of speech. Ideas don't emerge from a vacuum. They can take time to coalesce. As Brandeis had written back in 1890, "All law is a dead letter without public opinion behind it. But law & public opinion interact—and they are both capable of being made." Just as Brandeis's ideas in *Whitney* were the culmination of thinking over the years, his eloquent prose was the result of editing and more editing. Brandeis's case files for *Ruthenberg* and *Whitney* contain one draft after another, with somewhat pedestrian language being crossed out and more vivid images being written in. The work went through the summer of 1926 and into the first weeks of May 1927, ending only a few days before the decision was handed down on May 16.

Brandeis's opinion in *Whitney* did become a chapter in the development of American speech law, but it was also a chapter in American labor history. It brought together two very different people—Brandeis and Whitney—whose lives followed strikingly dissimilar trajectories. He was an increasingly revered justice and advisor to many of the Washington political elite; she, a radical on the fringes of the American ideological spectrum. Still, they had more in common than that would suggest. They were both formed in significant part by their experiences of the labor movement and the drive for economic justice in the industrializing society of the United States. The attempts of many employers and legislators to stifle the efforts of workers who claimed a share of the country's resources, the reaction of many influential Americans to the plight of the poor, and the fight for economic justice were just as much a hallmark of the nation in the late nineteenth and early twentieth centuries as the redefinition of democracy and the battle for racial justice were in the second half of the twentieth century or the struggle for gay rights was in the early decades of the twenty-first. Economic inequality formed the background of the *Whitney* case, which cannot be understood except in that context. The drive to expand the meaning of free speech was inextricably tied to activists' involvement with labor. It was propelled further by World War I, when the Espionage and Sedition Acts and the prosecutions under them first alerted numerous Americans to the dangers of suppression of speech. While the Free Speech League had existed in the early twentieth century, most of the people who would become the backbone of the civil liberties movement had paid little or no attention to the matter of speech before the war began and Congress decided to limit permissible speech. The California criminal syndicalism law and other similar state laws were the direct descendants of the federal statutes, but they were also part of a concerted battle against the demands of labor.

The ACLU was another element in the societal context and grew out of it. Roger Baldwin, like Brandeis and Whitney, came from a comfortable and fairly conservative background and gradually moved to the left ideologically. As we have seen, he was among a large number of public figures who became prominent in the labor movement or the Socialist Party or both. His contribution and that of the organization he helped create demonstrate the importance of civil society to the development of American speech law.

Social scientists refer to the prevalence of "civil society" as one of the defining characteristics of the United States. "Civil society," or "nongovernmental organizations," consists of citizens who organize formally or informally outside the government because of shared interests. Their organizations exist to accomplish specific goals and are to be found in a space in between government and the economy. The term encompasses everything from religious congregations, Little League baseball teams, and neighborhood self-help groups to the small and large charities that are a constant of American life. The 37-million-member AARP is part of civil society; so is the handful of neighbors who form a book group. The United States government estimates that there are a million and a half registered nongovernmental organizations in the country. Many more, like the book groups, are unregistered. The National Organization for the Advancement of Colored People (NAACP) is a civil society organization; so is the ACLU, and so was the Garland Fund.

Some civil society organizations have had an enormous impact on American law. Legal segregation would no doubt have ended eventually in the United States without the activities of the NAACP, but it is clear that the series of cases challenging segregated schools that the organization took to the Supreme Court in the 1930s through the 1950s was crucial to the way the law changed in the middle of the twentieth century. Similarly, if the ACLU had not provided lawyers to appeal on Whitney's behalf and if the Garland Fund had not been available to bankroll the effort, it is entirely possible that the case would not have reached the Supreme Court for a second time and the Brandeis opinion would not have made its way into American law—at least not in the form and at the time it did. The way in which Americans react to societal change by creating organizations advocating various public policies is part of the *Whitney* story as well.

Brandeis's particular contribution to the development of speech law within this societal context was his drawing on thinking by himself and others to connect the need for speech with the requirements of democracy. He effectively brought together what had been the disparate approaches of Holmes and Chafee on the one side, and Hand on the other. As noted earlier, Holmes and Chafee were wedded to the idea that if a court found that specific speech comprised a clear and present danger, it could be punished—although Holmes added the idea of incitement in his *Abrams* dissent. Hand was equally insistent that only direct incitement—speech urging *immediate* criminal activity, along the lines of "Grab your guns and let's march on the capital"—was illegitimate. Brandeis retained the clear and present danger test but made it a test of imminence: mere counseling of a crime ("Good citizens should take their guns and march on the capital") was insufficient to prove danger, unless the threatened evil was so imminent that there was no time for persuasion. His extraordinary contribution lay in his wrestling with and then articulating the connection between speech and democracy, in eloquent language that both the legal expert and the layperson could understand. Brandeis saw free speech as a component of individual happiness, but his *Whitney* opinion emphasized the impossibility of maintaining a democratic society in the absence of free speech. If a nation adopted Brandeis's formulation it would be able to prohibit or criminalize almost no speech, making the United States' approach to public speech a uniquely permissive one. And that, eventually, was what the Supreme Court and the nation whose laws it interpreted did. In 1927, however, Brandeis, and Justice Holmes, were still in the Court's minority.

Given its powerful defense of the right to speech, one might reasonably assume that Brandeis's opinion in *Whitney* was a dissent. It was not. It was a concurrence, which is an opinion written by a justice who agrees with the majority's decision but not with some or all of the reasoning behind it. Here Brandeis agreed with the majority's bottom line that the conviction had to be upheld, but he disagreed with the majority's conclusion that the law was constitutional and well within the legislature's powers no matter what the facts on the ground were. In the final paragraphs of the concurrence, Brandeis noted that the California constitution gave the state legislature the power to enact emergency legislation. That did not necessarily mean the criminal syndicalism law was legitimate under the federal Constitution, he said. The rights of free speech and assembly were so fundamental that a defendant had to be given the opportunity to question whether, when such a statute was enacted, "there actually did exist . . . a clear danger; whether the danger, if any, was imminent; and whether the evil apprehended was one so substantial as to justify the stringent restriction interposed by the legislature." In order to assess the constitutionality of the law as such and the constitutionality of the law as applied to a particular defendant, in other words, one had to know what the facts on the ground were both when the law was passed and when the act with which the defendant was charged occurred. The state wasn't necessarily correct in its assessment of a danger. A legislature's declaration that certain speech or assembly presented a public danger was only the opening of a conversation, not its conclusion.

Whitney, however, had not made that argument in the trial court. She did not ask the judge or jury to assess whether a real danger existed. There is of course no way of knowing whether the death of O'Connor and the lesser abilities of the ill-prepared Coghlan made all the difference here, but Brandeis was left with the fact that the argument had not been presented. "On the other hand, there was evidence on which the court or jury might have found that such danger existed." The jury should have been charged with making that factual determination. Brandeis rejected the majority's assumption that "assembling with a political party, formed to advocate the desirability of a proletarian revolution by mass action at some date necessarily far in the future," was not protected by the Constitution. Nonetheless, the trial court did hear testimony "which tended to establish the existence of a conspiracy, on the part of members of the International [*sic*] Workers of the World, to commit present serious crimes; and likewise to show that such a conspiracy would be furthered by the activity of the society of which Miss Whitney was a member." In the absence of a contention by Whitney that the testimony did not establish a clear and present danger, Brandeis felt unable to hold that the conviction was mistaken.

That may be a difficult position for many to understand, after reading Brandeis's paean to freedom of speech. He, however, had shown and would continue to show throughout his judicial career that he felt the power of the Supreme Court should be a limited one. Brandeis was a man of principle, and one of those principles was judicial restraint. Both as an attorney and as a jurist he had been appalled by what he saw as the undue activism by conservative Supreme Court justices, who reached out to strike down laws to which they were ideologically opposed. Courts were made to interpret laws, not make policy, he believed. That illuminated his approach to judging; it even, on occasion, led him to vote to uphold laws of which he clearly disapproved. If judicial self-restraint meant that judges had to vote against their political predilections when a case came before them, then they were doing no more than their duty. If democracy and the separation of powers were to survive, jurisdictional rules had to be followed meticulously. "My, how I detest that man's ideas," Justice George Sutherland, one of Brandeis's conservative colleagues on the Court, wrote. "But he is one of the greatest technical lawyers I have ever known."

Appeals courts do not normally overturn convictions for reasons that have not been raised by the defendants themselves in the courts below. Brandeis was not about to break that rule. In addition, he believed strongly that the federal judiciary should give the states full rein to experiment with legislation they considered wise. Federal courts were meant to intervene only if there was no question about the unconstitutionality of a state statute. As we will see, he did not think that Anita Whitney should be put behind bars, but he felt constrained by the boundaries of judicial power as he viewed them.

That left Anita Whitney still at risk. Whatever qualms Brandeis may have felt at voting to uphold her conviction did her no good at all. "I am not surprised" at the decision, Whitney commented. She had been waiting for it in a cottage in Carmel, gardening and caring for her mother, who was ill and partially blind. Once the Supreme Court ruled, she told the press, "I have no plans. My plans will probably be made up for me now."

It looked as if those plans would include living in a prison that, ironically enough, Whitney had helped build. The women's dormitory at San Quentin was so crowded that some inmates had to sleep on the floors, and Whitney had led a movement to have it replaced by a roomier new building that overlooked San Pablo Bay. It was due to be completed only months after she would begin her prison stay. She began to prepare herself mentally to inhabit it.

Neylan, though, was not ready to give up. C. C. Young, a progressive Republican, had beaten Governor Richardson in the 1926 Republican primary and had gone on to win in the general election. Neylan wanted Whitney to ask Governor Young, whom he knew and had actively supported during Young's gubernatorial campaign, for a pardon. She refused. "To ask the Governor to pardon me would be to admit I had done something wrong," she told the press. "I shall never do that." Just as she had in earlier years, she tried to turn attention to the plight of others; this time, to Nicola Sacco and Bartolomeo Vanzetti, two radicals who had been convicted of murder in a controversial Massachusetts case and who had been sentenced to die. Whitney, like Brandeis, clearly believed in the importance of educating the citizenry, and she was glad to use the press in order to do it. "My case is of little importance," she said to the journalists. "Compared with Sacco and Vanzetti whose very lives are at stake, my difficulty is insignificant."

Neylan filed a pardon petition on her behalf nonetheless. He issued a press release to rebut the picture of Whitney as a wealthy woman, while patting himself on the back for handling her case. "Miss Whitney inherited a modest fortune, which she has largely dissipated in aiding the poor and advancing the cause of the lowly," he declared. "Miss Whitney's total expenditures during the last seven years in relation to her case have been less than $1500. Her counsel have served during the last seven years without compensation and will not and would not accept compensation."

His petition gained immediate widespread support. The ACLU mobilized letter writers and petition signers around the nation. U.S. senator Hiram Johnson, himself a former governor of California, joined Dean Orrin K. McMurray of the University of California Law School in writing to Young, "Her activities, aside from the associations charged in the offense, have been wholly charitable, generous and benevolent." Jane Addams and a colleague organized attendees at a national social work conference to add their voices. State senator Kehoe, who had introduced the criminal syndicalism law, told Young, "I have read the reporter's transcript in her case and am at a loss to understand how a verdict of guilty was secured." Ray Benjamin, the former state Republican committeeman who had actually drafted the law, gave the press a letter saying that the statute was never meant to be applied to someone like Whitney. Governor Young reported hearing from bankers, corporation lawyers, newspaper publishers, mayors, judges and ex-judges, educators, veterans, "agricultural leaders," "men of large business affairs," and "churches of every denomination." He asked for recommendations from the judges of the District Court of Appeal who had heard her case, and two of the three (the third was out of the country) recommended a pardon. Justice John F. Tyler, one of those judges, was condescending but supportive nonetheless: "I am of the opinion that she has already been sufficiently punished, and that the granting to this aged little woman a pardon would be an act of mercy . . . the history of Miss Whitney's life . . . shows that both before and subsequent to her trial she simply allowed herself to be misguided by listening to the vicious principles of that class which is primarily responsible for her unfortunate situation."

Perhaps most surprisingly, James G. Quinn, the trial court judge whose questionable rulings had done so much to produce Whitney's conviction, sent Young a letter calling Whitney "a lady of culture and refinement, and I can well imagine the suffering she has undergone during more than seven years which have elapsed since her conviction. . . . I believe that justice and the welfare of the state would be observed in this case if she was granted a pardon." The *Los Angeles Times* reported that Young, who had been the speaker of the California Assembly when the syndicalism bill was passed and had voted for it, was spending "all his spare time" on the appeal. "He has taken all the documents home and already has read the entire transcript" and was reading it again.

The result of his reading, and perhaps of all the communications, and certainly of Brandeis's opinion, soon became clear. On June 20, 1927,

Young granted Whitney an unconditional pardon. He issued a fifteen-page statement reviewing the facts of the case and referring to the "unrest and nervous tension" at the time of her arrest. "I do not believe it conceivable that today such a trial would take place, or a conviction be demanded even by the strongest adherents of the Criminal Syndicalism Act." He lambasted the decision to admit evidence about the activities of the Wobblies and opined that the trial might have ended quite differently had O'Connor lived to represent Whitney. Young devoted part of his pardon message to "Justice Brandeis on Free Speech," one of the sections in which he quoted Brandeis at length. Brandeis's concurrence in *Whitney*, Young added, was "one of the finest expressions of the kind produced during the present generation." He then concluded, "Miss Whitney, life-long friend of the unfortunate, is not in any true sense a 'criminal,' and to condemn her, at sixty years of age, to a felon's cell is an action which is absolutely unthinkable." Brandeis, vacationing in his Chatham, Massachusetts, summer home, wrote to Felix Frankfurter, "The pardon of Anita Whitney was a fine job."

Neylan issued a statement emphasizing that "I have no sympathy with Miss Whitney's political views. But, on the other hand, I believe profoundly in the right of every American citizen to hold and peaceably advocate any view they may see fit. . . . I am glad," he added, "the case is ended." Anita Whitney was free to get on with her life—which, as it turned out, would include a great deal of speech.

CHAPTER SEVEN

How Free Should Speech Be?

Justice Brandeis's concurrence in *Whitney* changed the course of American speech law. The Supreme Court's majority was not ready to follow him in 1927, but it did so not many years later. To a great extent, that took the government out of the business of deciding what speech is lawful. Some critics, however, question whether that is an entirely good thing in the United States of the twenty-first century. It is a critique that deserves to be examined.

We have already seen the philosophical and societal context in which Brandeis developed the thinking that led to his *Whitney* opinion. This chapter details the Supreme Court's gradual adoption of the Brandeis approach. There is then an exploration of the ways in which other nations deal with the right to speech. It leads to a discussion of why and how American speech jurisprudence has come to be unique. That is followed by a brief review of domestic critiques of the American system, and a discussion of some of the speech issues relevant to the United States of today.

Brandeis's reasoning was formally adopted by the Supreme Court in 1969, when it handed down a *per curiam* decision (an unsigned opinion for the Court) in the case of *Brandenburg v. Ohio*. Clarence Brandenburg, represented in the Court by the ACLU, was the leader of a Ku Klux Klan group in Ohio. He had invited the press to a Klan event at which a few hooded figures burned a cross and made anti-Semitic and antiblack comments. The film a reporter made of the event and the reporter's testimony at trial indicated that Brandenburg and others said that "there might have to be revengeance [*sic*] taken" if the government "continues to suppress the white, Caucasian race." Brandenburg was convicted under the Ohio criminal syndicalism statute, fined, and sentenced to prison for one to ten years. He appealed, and the Supreme Court held that a state law punishing "mere advocacy" and criminalizing assembling with others "merely to advocate" violence or criminal syndicalism "as a means of accomplishing industrial or political reform" violated the free speech clause. "Such a statute," the decision said, "falls within the condemnation of the First and Fourteenth Amendments. The contrary teaching of [the decision in] *Whitney v. California* . . . is therefore overruled." The Court's opinion essentially bypassed the clear and present danger test by leaving it unmentioned.

The Court's choice of a *per curiam* decision frequently indicates that the justices have found the case to be a particularly easy one. It seems likely that the reason it opted for that kind of decision in *Brandenburg* was that long before the Court formally overruled *Whitney* in 1969, Brandeis's concurrence and the thinking behind it had a substantial impact on the justices. In 1931, Chief Justice Charles Evans Hughes wrote for the Court's seven-person majority when it overturned the conviction of a 19-year-old woman who raised a red flag at a young people's summer camp (*Stromberg v. California*). As in *Whitney*, the petition to the Supreme Court was funded by the ACLU and, again as in *Whitney*, it revolved around a piece of red material. In *Stromberg*, the cloth was used to symbolize both the Soviet Union and the U.S. Communist Party. California law specifically outlawed display of a "red flag, banner or badge . . . as a sign, symbol or emblem of opposition to organized government or as an invitation or stimulus to anarchistic action or as an aid to propaganda that is of a seditious character." The Supreme Court considered that too vague and all-encompassing. "There is no question but that the State may . . . provide for the punishment of those who indulge in utterances which incite to violence and crime," the Chief Justice wrote. Hughes did not quote the *Whitney* concurrence. Nonetheless, he was clearly channeling Brandeis on the need for free speech in a democracy as well as incitement as the test for when it might be punished, for he added, "The maintenance of the opportunity for free political discussion to the end that government may be responsive to the will of the people and that changes may be obtained by lawful means, an opportunity essential to the security of the Republic, is a fundamental principle of our constitutional system." Free speech, in other words, enabled the citizenry to get the political system to do what the electorate thought it should do, and without violence. Justices Holmes and Brandeis were still on the Court and voted with Hughes in the case. (Holmes would retire in 1932; Brandeis, in 1939.)

The Court continued to chip away at the logic behind the majority decision in *Whitney*. In 1937 it overturned the conviction of a man charged under the Oregon criminal syndicalism law with helping to organize a public meeting arranged by the Communist Party, in yet another appeal sponsored by the ACLU (*De Jonge v. Oregon*). "Peaceable assembly for lawful discussion cannot be made a crime," Chief Justice Hughes held, again speaking for the Court. "The holding of meetings for peaceable political action cannot be proscribed." Six years later, in 1943, Justice Frank Murphy wrote the Court's opinion in *Schneiderman v. United States*, which overturned the denaturalization of a citizen who belonged to the Workers (Communist) Party of America. Murphy cited Brandeis in *Whitney* and stated that the criterion for differentiating between advocacy and incitement was whether there was "opportunity for general discussion and the calm process of thought and reason."

Even during the McCarthy period of the 1950s, when the Court once again upheld prosecutions for what amounted to radical opinions, it continued to pay tribute to the Brandeis concurrence. The 1940 federal Smith Act, based on the New York criminal anarchy law under which Benjamin Gitlow was convicted, criminalized advocacy of the violent overthrow of the government. In 1951 Chief Justice Fred M. Vinson penned the court's opinion in *Dennis v. United States* that legitimized prosecutions under the Act, but he nonetheless wrote, "Although no case subsequent to Whitney and Gitlow has expressly overruled the majority opinions in those cases, there is little doubt that subsequent opinions have inclined toward the Holmes-Brandeis rationale." Justice Frankfurter, concurring, and Justice William O. Douglas, dissenting, both cited Brandeis's *Whitney* opinion. The Court subsequently overturned a number of Smith Act convictions, holding that advocating violent overthrow of the government, in the absence of incitement, could not be punished (*Yates v. United States*, 1957).

In 1964 the Court struck down an Alabama court's decision that the *New York Times* had committed libel when it published an advertisement by civil rights activists that contained misstatements about a local public official (*New York Times v. Sullivan*). Writing for a unanimous court, Justice William Brennan quoted Brandeis's "'those who won our independence . . . believed that public discussion is a political duty,'" and declared that there was "a profound national commitment to the principle that debate on public issues should be uninhibited, robust, and wide-open." Justice Arthur Goldberg, concurring along with Justice Douglas and also quoting Brandeis in *Whitney*, wrote, "Our national experience teaches that repressions breed hate and 'that hate menaces stable government.'"

By the 1970s, after the *Brandenburg* decision was handed down, Brandeis's language was regularly cited and quoted by both the Supreme Court and lower courts in cases dealing with speech and press. It was referred to in 1971 in *Cohen v. California*, when Justice John Marshall Harlan said for the Court that "the constitutional right of free expression . . . is designed and intended to remove governmental restraints from the area of public discussion, putting the decision as to what views shall be voiced largely into the hands of each of us, in the hope that use of such freedom will ultimately produce a more capable citizenry and more perfect polity and in the belief that no other approach would comport with the premise of individual dignity and choice upon which our system rests." The court again cited the *Whitney* concurrence's "public discussion is a political duty" language in 1976, in the campaign finance case of *Buckley v. Valeo*. Justice Brennan's opinion for the Court in *Texas v. Johnson* (1987), striking down the conviction of a man who burned the American flag as a protest against policies of the Reagan administration, quoted Brandeis's paragraph about education through good speech being the cure for bad speech.

. That may appear to be a long list but in fact those are just a few of the cases relying on the thinking behind the *Whitney* concurrence, which became no less influential during the next decades. As of 2015, Brandeis's concurrence had been referred to by the Supreme Court in close to 100 cases and by state and lower federal courts in over 250. It had become a canon of American law, and the basis for the uniquely permissive American approach to speech. It was used both to uphold and to strike down laws abridging speech, in a variety of areas of the law. The Supreme Court cited it, for example, in overturning restrictions on the right to an abortion (*Planned Parenthood v. Casey*, 1992), striking down a law prohibiting federal employees from accepting pay for speeches or

articles (*United States v. National Treasury Employees Union*, 1995), upholding the right of the media to publish the contents of an intercepted telephone conversation (*Bartnicki v. Vopper*, 2001), declaring that the Second
Amendment's right to bear arms is binding on the states as well as the
federal government (*McDonald v. City of Chicago*, 2010), and overturning
a federal statute penalizing anyone who falsely claimed to have been
awarded a military honor (*United States v. Alvarez*, 2012). Both the majority and the minority referred to the *Whitney* concurrence in a 2010 case
validating a statute outlawing provision of services to organizations the
government had declared to be guilty of terrorism (*Holder v. Humanitarian Law Project*). The four justices dissenting from the Supreme Court's
holding in the election finance case of *McCutcheon v. Federal Election Commission* (2014), which allowed almost unlimited money to flow to candidates for federal office, cited Brandeis's statement in *Whitney* that free
speech was "essential to effective democracy."

In short, the Brandeis language has become among the most often
cited passages in American constitutional law. Chief Justice Hughes
noted in his *The Supreme Court of the United States* that dissenting opinions
are "an appeal to the brooding spirit of the law." The recognition that
dissents are markers laid down in the hope that the Supreme Court will
change its mind can apply equally, as *Whitney* demonstrates, to concurring opinions. Legal scholars have called the justice's opinion in *Whitney*
"arguably the most important essay ever written, on or off the bench,
on the meaning of the first amendment" (Vincent Blasi) and "the central twentieth-century judicial text in the American free speech canon"
(Clyde Spillenger). The late *New York Times* Supreme Court reporter
and legal scholar Anthony Lewis considered it "the greatest judicial
statement of the case for freedom of speech."

The notion that Brandeis wrote into American law is a particularly
striking one: bad speech deserves the same protection as good speech.
That is not because bad speech is useful to society. Instead, the justifications are that permitting bad speech is a lesser evil than giving the government the power to decide what speech is legitimate; responding to
bad speech involves citizens in the political process, as they should be in
any democracy worthy of the name, and furthers their development as
human beings; and outlawing bad speech merely drives it underground
where it cannot be challenged and rebutted.

Part of the Court's responsibility in speech cases, according to Brandeis, is to remind Americans what their political philosophy is, and why. *Whitney* and its predecessors demonstrate that it is a responsibility that the Court does not always fulfill. Nonetheless, the Court usually gets there in the end.

What "there" means, however, is a subject that is constantly up for debate. *Brandenburg* and subsequent decisions make it clear that *political* speech is to be as unfettered as possible. Exactly how far that doctrine extends, and its implications for other kinds of speech, is less obvious. The difficulty is exemplified by the phenomenon of hate speech, which is speech that denigrates on the basis of race, religion, ethnicity, gender, sexual orientation, or national origin. Should it be allowed, for example, when its object is a particular person or group? What if someone says that no woman, or Hispanic, or African American can possibly understand politics, and they should not be permitted to hold public office? However noxious, that statement about certain groups is part of political discourse and is clearly permissible under the *Brandenburg* rule. What if the comment is directed not at a group but at a particular person, as in "Senator Smith is a Mormon, and Mormons are an unChristian cult, and no Mormon should ever be president of the United States"? Again, that would be allowable—but not in many other nations. As has been stated, no other country takes the United States' permissive approach to speech. In assessing the implications of Brandeis's reasoning in *Whitney*, it is helpful to understand what other nations do, and why. The difference is particularly notable in the area of hate speech, as a comparison between the Canadian and American approaches demonstrates.

In the late 1970s John Ross Taylor and the Western Guard Party handed out cards inviting their fellow Canadians to call a Toronto telephone number. People who dialed in found themselves listening to virulent anti-Semitic messages. Acting under section 13(1) of the Canadian Human Rights Act, which prohibits telephone messages likely to expose a person or persons to "hatred or contempt" because of their race or religion, the Canadian Human Rights Commission ordered Taylor and the party to stop the messages. They did not, and were convicted of contempt of court. Taylor was sentenced to one year's imprisonment, and the party was fined $5,000. They appealed to the Canadian Supreme Court, arguing that section 13(1) violated the freedom of expression guaranteed by the Canadian Charter of Rights and Freedoms.

The court found it "unarguable that freedom of expression is held especially dear in a free and democratic society" and that it provides "the bedrock for the discovery of truth and consensus in all facets of human life, though perhaps most especially in the political arena." And, the court added in a statement that would have fit comfortably into Brandeis's *Whitney* opinion, "this freedom allows individuals to direct and shape their personal development, thereby promoting the respect for individual dignity and autonomy that is crucial to (among other things) a meaningful operation of the democratic process." There was no question that section 13(1) did impinge on freedom of expression, the judges said. Nonetheless, "hate propaganda contributes little to the aspirations of Canadians or Canada in either the quest for truth, the promotion of individual self-development or the protection and fostering of a vibrant democracy where the participation of all individuals is accepted and encouraged." Section 13(1) was therefore "rationally connected to the aim of restricting activities antithetical to the promotion of equality and tolerance in society." The punishments were upheld.

Taylor and the party appealed not only to the Canadian courts but to the United Nations Human Rights Committee as well. The Committee decided that "the opinions which Mr. Taylor seeks to disseminate through the telephone system clearly constitute the advocacy of racial or religious hatred which Canada has an obligation under article 20(2) of the Covenant to prohibit." The reference was to the International Covenant on Civil and Political Rights, a mainstay of international human rights law. Article 19 says in part, "Everyone shall have the right to freedom of expression. . . . The exercise of the right[s] . . . carries with it special duties and responsibilities" and is subject to restrictions that are "necessary . . . for respect of the rights or reputations of others." Article 20(2) adds, "Any advocacy of national, racial or religious hatred that constitutes incitement to discrimination, hostility or violence shall be prohibited by law."

The "rights of others" was at issue in another case that arose in the late 1970s, but this one was in the United States. It involved a planned demonstration by a neo-Nazi party in the Chicago suburb of Skokie, home to a large number of Jewish Holocaust survivors and their families. In language reminiscent of the Hitler era, the party's platform called for the "final solution of the Jewish question," a "National Eugenics Commission . . . for the elimination of all racial impurities," and "repatriation of all American Negroes to their African homeland." Its members sought a permit for a demonstration at the Skokie town hall. They intended to wear their Nazi-era swastika-covered uniforms during the demonstration and to carry signs such as "Free Speech for the White Man." The Holocaust survivors and other Jewish residents told Skokie officials that the sight of uniformed Nazis on the streets of their village would subject them to great psychological harm. Skokie denied the permit to the neo-Nazis, and the ACLU agreed to represent the party in court, asserting what it saw as the party's right to communicate its ideas. The question for the ACLU, as it had been for Brandeis, was not whether the party's ideas were heinous. The ACLU's executive director was a German-born Jew; the main ACLU lawyer in the case was Jewish. The issue for them was whether the government should have the power to decide which ideas were and were not acceptable.

The case was heard by federal district court judge Bernard Decker. Citing Brandeis's opinion in *Whitney*, Judge Decker ruled that the neo-Nazis did have a right to demonstrate. "The question," he wrote, "is not whether there are some ideas that are completely unacceptable in a civilized society. Rather the question is which danger is greater: the danger that allowing the government to punish 'unacceptable' ideas will lead to suppression of ideas that are merely uncomfortable to those in power; or the danger that permitting free debate on such unacceptable ideas will encourage their acceptance rather than discouraging them by revealing their pernicious quality." His answer was that the danger of suppression was the greater evil.

The differences between the decisions in Canada and the United States are striking. Both societies cherish the right to speak, which is enshrined in their basic laws. What was permissible in the United States, however, was punishable some miles to the north. In fact, the kind of hate speech practiced by the neo-Nazi party was illegal in just about every other country in the world.

Argentina, Australia, Brazil, Cameroon, Chile, China, Colombia,

Cuba, Denmark, France, Germany, Great Britain, Mexico, Netherlands, Niger, Senegal, Spain, Sweden, and Venezuela are among the countries that criminalize forms of hate speech. The laws of the Czech Republic, Denmark, Israel, Jordan, Madagascar, Mauritius, Panama, Portugal, Sudan, Sweden, and Syria prohibit defamation of religious groups. In Great Britain, a person who uses abusive or intentionally harassing language about race, religion, or sexual orientation can be fined or sentenced to prison. France specifically outlaws public display of the kind of Nazi uniforms that the American group proposed to wear in Skokie. Hungarian law makes it illegal to display the swastika. The German Criminal Code bans attacks on "the human dignity of others" that are likely to breach the peace because of "inciting to hatred against part of the population" or "insulting, maliciously making them contemptible, or defaming them." That includes displaying Nazi symbols such as the swastika.

Similarly, India's Penal Code makes it illegal to promote, through speech or pictures, "disharmony or feelings of enmity, hatred or ill-will between different religious, racial, language or regional groups" or to suggest that "members of any religious, racial, language or regional group or caste or community" cannot be good citizens or should be deprived of their rights as citizens. Argentina makes "anyone who in whatever way encourages or incites to persecution or hatred of a person or group of persons of a particular religion, ethnic origin or colour for reasons of their race, religion, nationality or political views" subject to punishment. Anyone who "publicly or by any means suitable for dissemination incites any person to hatred or contempt . . . against one or more persons by reason of the colour of their skin, their race, religion, or national or ethnic origin" in Uruguay can be imprisoned. Namibia's Racial Discrimination Prohibition Act of 1911 and New Zealand's Race Relations Act of 1971 are among the many national statutes that criminalize incitement to racial disharmony. The South African constitution declares, "Everyone has the right to freedom of expression" but the right "does not extend to . . . advocacy of hatred that is based on race, ethnicity, gender or religion, and that constitutes incitement to cause harm."

The same kind of approach to hate speech is found in many international human rights instruments. The United States has signed the

International Covenant on Civil and Political Rights that was cited in the Canadian case, as have over 150 other countries ranging alphabetically from Afghanistan to Zimbabwe. Other such treaties include, for example, the 1965 International Convention on the Elimination of All Forms of Racial Discrimination. It condemns all "ideas or theories of superiority of one race or group of persons of one colour or ethnic origin, or which attempt to justify or promote racial hatred and discrimination in any form" and calls upon nations that have signed the Convention to criminalize all dissemination of such ideas, provision of any assistance to racist activities, and organizations that promote and incite racial discrimination.

That sampling is sufficient to demonstrate that in the field of speech, and particularly hate speech, the United States is the outlier. What accounts for the difference? And is the American approach wise?

The early history of the First Amendment was discussed in chapter 2. Fearful of the potentially great power of the federal government, the writers of the amendment prohibited that government from acting at all in the area of speech. The words of the First Amendment have never been changed on paper, but the Supreme Court has altered them nonetheless. The amendment, as we have seen, says "Congress shall make no law . . . abridging the freedom of speech." In spite of the words "no law," the amendment was interpreted in the 1919 Espionage Act decisions to allow just such a law. That was the first change. Then, in 1925, *Gitlow v. United States* extended the prohibition to the states. (In the following decades, the Court gradually extended the guarantees of the rest of the Bill of Rights to the states.) No one at the time, however, doubted that the states still had the power to criminalize some speech. Justice Sanford in fact specifically said in *Gitlow* that states could punish speech that was "inimical to the public welfare, tending to corrupt public morals, incite to crime, or disturb the public peace." The Court's interpretations of the First Amendment have effectively altered the speech clause so that it now means that "Congress *and the states* shall make no law . . . abridging the freedom of speech *except when they and the Supreme Court consider such a law to be permissible."*

The result is that what are still the words-on-paper of the First

Amendment no longer convey its reality. At the same time, there is no general agreement on exactly what the words do mean, or why. There was no national conversation when the amendment was adopted about what speech should and should not be permitted in a democratic society. Similarly, there was no such conversation among most policy-makers, or within the population at large, when the Supreme Court's interpretive changes took place. In addition, while Brandeis laid out the rationale for permitting the greatest possible latitude to political speech, and while other legal thinkers were part of a wider discussion in the 1920s, there are two questions of relevance today that even they did not address. That brings us to the second part of the answer about why American speech jurisprudence is singular.

The first issue left unaddressed by the conversation in the 1920s is, given the right of people in a democracy to free speech, what are their responsibilities in exercising it? Brandeis did speak of one kind of responsibility: the responsibility of citizens to participate in political discussion. While he mentioned the importance of individual autonomy and development as one reason for the speech right, he nonetheless emphasized the positive utility of the individual's thinking to the larger society. He did not consider the potential harm to other individuals of hurtful speech. To put it somewhat differently: if there is a responsibility to speak, might there also be a responsibility not to speak? That is the consideration that lies behind the jurisprudence of other nations, which emphasize rights as being exercised within the context of a different responsibility to the community: the obligation of each member of it to treat other members with dignity and respect.

The way various societies view speech rights can be explained in large part by their distinctive histories. The unique American approach is one that could have been generated only in a highly heterogeneous society long committed to the rule of law and the protection of rights. The American electorate of the early twentieth century was not as diverse or as welcoming of diversity as it would become 100 years later—it would have been unthinkable for the president of the United States to hold a Jewish seder or a Muslim *iftar* in the White House, as is now the norm—but as a nation of immigrants it had already incorporated into its psychology as well as its ideology the necessity to tolerate differences. Adherence to a set of legal norms, and the idea that disputes had to be handled only through legal processes, had become embedded in popular culture—what we might describe as the societal DNA. That is why Brandeis could be unfazed by the communists' verbal threats of radical change, or why Judge Decker could be equally undaunted by the neo-Nazis' ideology, unacceptable as both jurists considered the two sets of beliefs. When a democracy is composed of people from many different backgrounds living in a wide range of environments spread over a large swath of territory, it will inevitably hear the expression of a multiplicity of ideas. Both Brandeis and Decker were used to the great variety of opinions endemic to such a heterogeneous electorate. Moreover, neither judge considered fringe groups a real threat to American society, nor did they expect the groups to violate legal norms or to gain much of a following if they attempted to do so. They could therefore conclude that there was a greater likelihood of harm resulting from the suppression of distasteful speech than there was from allowing it to be heard.

Other countries, with histories variously of less experience with heterogeneity and more experience of mass violence, and with their basic laws written at later historical moments than the American constitution, have reached a different conclusion. They have seen at first hand the undermining of social cohesion that can be caused in their nations by unbridled speech. It would have been naïve to expect that a constitution or speech laws adopted after the Holocaust or South African apartheid or any of the other human-made violent tragedies of the twentieth century would parallel those enacted far earlier. History and the resultant societal culture, then, are largely responsible for making American speech jurisprudence unique.

The second issue that was left unaddressed in the United States in the 1920s and thereafter was whether and how restrictions on speech enacted by the states should be different from limitations imposed by the federal government. There is general agreement that the states' obligation to provide for the general welfare includes the power to regulate, for example, libel, obscenity, and pornography—but why should that be true? How do those forms of speech differ from the kind of political speech championed by Brandeis? It is easy enough to say that only speech that is a useful addition to the political debate should be unfettered, and that libel and such add nothing to it. Who or what, though, should be empowered to make the decision that some speech is useless or potentially harmful, and on what basis? After all, the California legislature, its courts, and the U.S. Supreme Court had made exactly that determination about Anita Whitney's speech. What ought to be the limits of speech, and on the government's power to determine what they should be?

That brings us to consider the conditions of democracy. The United States relies on Brandeis's assertion that almost unlimited speech is crucial in a democracy and that the free flow of ideas will inevitably be damaged if the government is allowed to decide who shall be permitted to say what. Other nations look at human history and argue that unfettered speech has caused a level of misery and injustice that they cannot allow to be repeated. They view speech as part of a democracy but, as well, as a potential threat to it. That is why Germany and France, for example, forbid the utterance of some Nazi speech. Both want to safeguard their societies from the kinds of horrors that occurred during the Nazi period. They are uncertain of how well their countries would survive unregulated fascist speech.

The problem of whether it could happen here—that is, whether the United States enjoys a system so stable that it is unlikely to be threatened by a system of free speech—is central to the discussion. The question also could be framed as one about whether a democratic society can afford *not* to have a system of free speech: whether the kind of informed decisions "we the people" are called upon to make in a democracy are possible in the absence of a free flow of ideas. The preconditions for making certain that unfettered speech serves a society well would seem to include the rule of law and a written constitution, as well as the existence of private groups devoted to maintaining the system of free speech. American speech jurisprudence assumes a societal consensus that dissent and any reactions to it will be expressed through legally acceptable channels, and that any changes in the political and economic system will come through evolution rather than revolution.

One other vital factor in a democracy is an independent judiciary. The unique position of the Supreme Court is a crucial part of the *Whitney* story. No other nation's high court has as much power to impact public policy. That power is particularly important when the elected branches of the federal and state governments infringe on the civil liberties of the people. There have been numerous times in American history—the *Whitney* case took place during one of them—when the electorate has perceived itself as being under threat and the government has acted to stifle dissenting voices. Historian Richard Hofstadter, surveying instances of repression throughout American history, concluded that the nation frequently suffers from what he labeled "The Paranoid Style in American Politics." Anthony Lewis made a similar statement in the years after the tragedy of September 11, 2001. The American people are apt to react to perceived dangers from abroad, he noted, by acting as if "civil liberties must be sacrificed to protect the country from foreign threats." "We Americans do panic really well," *New York Times* columnist Frank Bruni commented some years later during the Ebola scare of 2014. That was certainly true in the post–World War I period when Anita Whitney and so many of her fellow radicals were put on trial.

The Supreme Court, as we have seen, is very much part of the public it serves (as, of course, are the lower courts). Its members live through the same events and can be prey to the same fears. The phenomenon was evident in the 1919 speech decisions it handed down. When the Court steps back from the emotions of the moment and reminds the citizenry of the ideals embodied in the Constitution, however, as Holmes did in *Abrams* and *Gitlow*, Brandeis did in *Whitney*, and the entire court did in *Brandenburg v. Ohio*, it can both safeguard minorities and serve an educative function. Thomas Reed Powell, another major legal scholar of the twentieth century, wrote in a review of Chafee's *Freedom of Speech*, "Nine men in Washington cannot hold a nation to ideals which it is determined to betray. Whether justice is done to the particular defendant is important, but in the long run less important than whether a nation does justice to itself."

The history of the First Amendment suggests that, at least where speech is concerned, the nation's ideals are somewhat less than clear, and yet the Supreme Court has played a primary role in limning them.

A number of questions can be asked about American speech jurisprudence today. Some have been asked over the years by American critics; others stem from more recent controversial Supreme Court decisions; still others have been raised by technological advances.

What is perhaps the sharpest criticism of American speech jurisprudence and the Brandeis and ACLU model comes from the Critical Legal Studies school of thought. Its proponents, primarily a number of law professors, argue that the ideas and doctrines that underlie American law are merely extensions of a political system that legitimizes injustice and the dominance of American society by groups such as white people, men, and the wealthy. Their critique says in part that by permitting what legal scholar Mari Matsuda and others have labeled "words that wound," the law effectively silences or penalizes civic participation by and full citizenship for other groups such as racial and ethnic minorities, women, gays and lesbians, employees, low-income people, and persons with disabilities. Similarly, Feminist Legal Theory focuses on the effect of pornography and verbal sexual harassment on women. Critics such as Catharine MacKinnon and Andrea Dworkin have argued that the concept of free speech has been misused to allow sexually explicit material that subordinates women, condones violence against them, and denies them full equality at home, in the workplace, and in society at large. Does permitting "words that wound" and sexually explicit language conflict with the democratic goals of equality and inclusiveness?

A second critique has emerged as a result of the late-twentieth and early-twenty-first century decisions by the Supreme Court, which relied in some measure on Brandeis's reasoning, striking down laws designed to regulate the flow of money into political campaigns. The Court has ruled in cases such as *Citizens United v. Federal Election Commission* (2010) that contributions to political campaigns and expenditures to publicize a candidate's views are a form of speech, and so the free speech clause prohibits the government from limiting the amount of money that can be contributed to and spent on election campaigns. Those decisions have generated criticism from people who argue that money is not speech and that the democratic process is in danger of being undermined by the infusion of large amounts of money from wealthy people and groups. If we say that the expenditure of money is speech, have we made a mockery of the democracy that free speech is meant to safeguard and enhance?

The development of the Internet has raised another set of questions about American speech laws. Internet bullying has become a societal problem. It has resulted in a number of widely covered adolescent suicides, and research suggests that the bullying phenomenon is fairly widespread. Is the answer a limitation on speech, or better education about bullying and the importance of civility? Internet speech that is potentially incendiary but perhaps not immediately inciteful and that therefore cannot be punished under current law raises yet another issue. An example might be a post that says, "Abortion is murder; Dr. Smith performs abortions; here is his address," or "Councilwoman Jones is threatening to vote to take away the guns we all need to protect ourselves, and she lives at 461 Elm Drive." Still another concern comes from the national security and law enforcement communities, which point to the problem of the spread of terrorist messages on the Internet.

In addition, the Web has made incursions into the zone of personal privacy that has historically contributed to civic courage and political participation. In the past, people could participate in public discussions and then retire to the relative anonymity of their homes. The Internet and the availability of large amounts of information about almost everyone has severely limited privacy and anonymity. There may be ways in which the rights to speech and privacy sometimes conflict.

Interestingly enough, Justice Brandeis is as renowned for his thinking about privacy as he is for his work on free speech. In 1890, he and his law partner Samuel Warren were outraged at what they saw as the intrusive newspaper coverage given to what they thought of as private events, including the marriage of Warren's daughter. Their response was an article entitled "The Right to Privacy" that was published in the *Harvard Law Review*. It made the phrase "the right to be let alone" part of American political discourse and has been called "perhaps the most influential law journal piece ever published." Harvard Law School's Dean Roscoe Pound later credited it with "nothing less than add[ing] a chapter to our law."

The article combined the issue of privacy with a conception of the law as a changing entity, arguing that new inventions with the potential for violations of privacy had to be brought under law: "instantaneous photographs and newspaper enterprise have invaded the sacred precincts of private and domestic life; and numerous mechanical devices threaten to make good the prediction that 'what is whispered in the closet shall be proclaimed from the house-tops.'" Brandeis and Warren equated the right to privacy with "the right to one's personality" and asserted that individuals should be able to seek an award of damages from the courts if that right was abridged by other persons or by institutions.

They carefully differentiated what they saw as private life from public life. "The right to privacy does not prohibit any publication of matter which is of public or general interest," they wrote. While an ordinary individual's "peculiarities of manner and person" should be protected, such

> peculiarities ... may acquire a public importance, if found in a candidate for public office. Some further discrimination is necessary, therefore, than to class facts or deeds as public or private according to a standard to be applied to the fact or deed *per se*. To publish of a modest and retiring individual that he suffers from an impediment in his speech or that he cannot spell correctly, is an unwarranted, if not an unexampled, infringement of his rights, while to state and comment on the same characteristics found in a would-be congressman could not be regarded as beyond the pale of propriety.

Such reticence may seem quaint in the twenty-first-century world of social media, selfies, and reality television, when the most intimate details of many people's lives are regularly made public. To the Brandeis of 1890, however, "The common law has always recognized a man's house as his castle, impregnable, often, even to its own officers engaged in the execution of its commands." Warren and Brandeis advocated allowing people whose privacy was invaded to sue for damages. They went so far as to suggest that the government might punish what they considered to be extreme cases, where a newspaper published personal information about a private individual after being requested not to do so. It is worth noting that the article says nothing about criminalizing speech, as distinguished from articles in the press, and that it is impossible to know whether criminalization of such publications would have been favored by Brandeis in subsequent years, after he "thought ... through" speech. It is also notable that Brandeis and Warren recognized the difficulty of distinguishing the private sphere from the public one and of defining what speech is societally useful. Brandeis made it clear years later, when the Supreme Court heard the 1931 case of *Near v. Minnesota*, that he was particularly concerned about protecting speech having to do with public affairs.

The *Saturday Press*, published by Jay Near, had been enjoined from publication under a Minnesota statute aimed against periodicals that were "malicious, scandalous and defamatory." Minnesota acted after the newspaper accused public officials by name of being participants in a gambling ring. The publication was also noted for its virulent anti-Semitism, and many Court-watchers expected Brandeis, by then known not only as the Court's first Jewish member but as the leader of American Zionism as well, to take the side of the state. But when the case was argued before the Court, Brandeis interrupted the Minnesota deputy attorney general's presentation. It was common knowledge, Brandeis declared, that "just such criminal combinations" involving public officials did exist, "to the shame of some of our cities." Brandeis could not tell whether this was true in Minnesota, but he did know that Near and his partner had exposed what they believed to be such a combination. "Now, is that not a privileged communication, if there ever was one?" he asked. "How else can a community secure protection from that sort of thing, if people are not allowed to engage in free discussion in such matters? . . . You are dealing here not with a sort of scandal too often appearing in the press, and which ought not to appear to the interest of any one, but with a matter of prime interest to every American citizen."

The attorney general responded that citizens ought to be concerned if the allegations were correct, but that in this instance they had been defamatory. "Of course there was defamation," Brandeis replied. "You cannot disclose evil without naming the doers of evil . . . how can such a campaign [against corruption] be conducted except by persistence and continued iteration?" Brandeis, who had battled a corrupt Massachusetts legislature during his years as a Boston lawyer, praised the publishers for their "campaign to rid the city of certain evils." "So they say," the lawyer commented. "Yes, of course," Brandeis agreed, "so they say. They went forward with a definite program and certainly they acted with great courage. . . . Now, if that campaign was not privileged, if that is not one of the things for which the press chiefly exists, then for what does it exist?"

Brandeis did not write an opinion in *Near*, simply adding his name to Chief Justice Charles Evans Hughes's opinion for the Court, which struck down the statute by a vote of 5–4. His comments during oral argument, however, indicate that he was still thinking of the press right in the context of the good achieved by giving public discourse the widest possible latitude. It is possible to agree with him about that necessity and yet acknowledge that the Brandeis doctrine does not provide answers to some of the questions posed earlier.

As we have seen, Brandeis was a champion of the idea of a living Constitution that responded to societal developments. It would have been impossible for him to imagine the conundrums created by the Internet or the ubiquity of television and the great advantage it gives to political discourse by individuals and corporations able to buy time for political advertisements on it. The twenty-first-century blurring of the boundaries between the personal and the political was similarly unthinkable. He and Samuel Warren referred in their privacy article to the difficulty of distinguishing between speech that is useful as a part of political debate and that which is not, but did not leave us with a test for differentiating useful speech from any other speech—and, indeed, perhaps there is no such thing as a bright line between them.

As mentioned earlier, the question of under what circumstances speech should be limited, and why, has not been addressed head-on. Occasionally various bodies have considered aspects of it. In passing the Smith Act of 1940, Congress decided that advocacy of violent overthrow of the government should be outlawed. The Supreme Court first agreed, as we have seen, and then changed its mind. State legislatures have enacted various laws criminalizing hate speech, and university campuses have attempted to regulate it. Some of those laws and regulations have survived judicial scrutiny; others have not. The federal Communications Decency Act of 1996 would have banned from the Internet any "indecent" materials that could be accessed by people under the age of 18. That section of the act was struck down by the Supreme Court, in the 1997 case of *Reno v. American Civil Liberties Union*, as unconstitutionally vague and as limiting access by adults to material such as literary works that included what a government bureaucrat might consider to be "indecent" content.

What is missing, in all the sporadic legislative efforts to respond to discomfort with particular kinds of speech, is a focused discussion by policymakers about the meaning and parameters of speech in the American democracy. Why is free speech important? Are all kinds of speech equally legitimate in a democracy? If not, how can the illegitimate ones be identified, and by whom or what? How can speech that is useful be differentiated from speech that is not? If some speech is to be labeled overly harmful and therefore subject to punishment, exactly how harmful must it be, and how can that be measured? If punishment is appropriate, should that take the form of criminal prosecution, or a civil suit for damages, or both? Would limitations on speech put us on a slippery slope that might result in stifling ultimately useful ideas, and is it wiser to fight hurtful speech with "good" speech? Should we be examining and working to change the underlying attitudes that lead some people to engage in hate speech rather than focusing on restricting the speech itself? The late twentieth and early twenty-first centuries have experienced critiques of American speech law unlike any seen at any other historical moments. The formal national commitment to unbridled political speech dates only to 1969 and *Brandenburg*, which in the arc of history is not particularly long at all. The commitment may be vulnerable.

We are left, then, with a multiplicity of questions. The overarching one, of course, is whether the circumstances of the twenty-first century should result in alterations to our speech jurisprudence. It is a dilemma that undoubtedly will be with us and part of the societal discourse for some time to come. The best society, Brandeis would argue, is one in which the government does not have the power to decide what ideas can be uttered and heard. It was his strong belief, based on his view of American history and political culture, that we can weather even the most undemocratic speech, and that it is best for us to absorb whatever hurts come from words that wound and whatever dangers come from speech that presents no immediate threat. Law professor Alan Dershowitz has provided an updated version of that approach: "It's not that I believe the exercise of the freedom of speech will always bring about good results; it's that I believe that the exercise of the power to censor will almost always bring about bad results. It's not that I believe the free marketplace of ideas will always produce truth; it's that I believe that the shutting down of that marketplace by government will prevent the possibility of truth."

Is this creed still the wisest one for American democracy, or is American free speech jurisprudence no more than an outmoded accident of the wording of the First Amendment and the role of the Supreme Court in interpreting it?

Epilogue

Anita Whitney never stopped exercising her right to speak. Another woman might have taken her seven-year ordeal as sufficient reason to retreat from public life, but Whitney was not that woman. In 1926, when her case was being considered by the Supreme Court for the second time, she mounted an attack on the miscegenation laws that existed across the southern part of the nation. "If a full-grown man and woman wish to live together as man and wife it is only decent to allow them to do it, no matter what their color," she declared at a San Francisco meeting of the National Woman's Party. Two years after her pardon, she was arrested in San Francisco when she and nine other Communists ignored police orders to stop demonstrating in front of the Chinese consulate, chanting anti-imperialist slogans and waving red banners. They had run afoul of the red flag law that would be tested before the Supreme Court in *Stromberg v. California* (see chapter 6). Undaunted, Whitney informed the press that the Communist Party was "the hope of the world" and added, "I have been told that my Communistic activities show ingratitude to Gov. Young for the pardon he accorded me. I deny that. . . . If I had not been innocent Gov. Young should not have pardoned me . . . as an American citizen I must do what I think is right. Freedom and equality are at the very basis of our government. The right of free expression is inalienable under our Constitution."

That was in July 1929. The following month, on the anniversary of the outbreak of World War I, Whitney was arrested at a Communist Party demonstration, carrying a placard that read, "August First is The International Day Against Imperialist War." In October she was among 500 Communists who were present at an open-air meeting in Oakland that was called on behalf of North Carolina mill workers who had been charged with murder during a labor protest. Nine of the other participants in the meeting were arrested for passing out handbills. Whitney followed the patrol wagon to the city hall and managed to post bail for all of them. She and they then returned to the site and continued their meeting.

Whitney never lost her faith that the combination of speech, direct action, and the political process would achieve progress. She was sometimes to be found in the early morning distributing leaflets outside railroad shops, at noon meetings outside cotton mills, at street meetings in San Francisco, or raising money for strike kitchens, all to challenge unfair labor practices and to get signatures so that Communist Party candidates for public office could be placed on the California state ballot. Throughout the 1930s and 1940s she ran for election as the party's candidate for state controller, the U.S. House of Representatives, and the U.S. Senate. She won more than 100,000 votes when she ran for state controller in 1934. Unfortunately for her, however, she had attested to the authenticity of signatures on her election petition that year, and she was subsequently convicted of having falsely certified them as genuine although at least some of the petitions had not been signed in her presence. Sentenced for that to 300 days in San Quentin or a $600 fine, she refused to pay. A nephew who was living with her persuaded the court to let him pay the fine, and Whitney was freed. The *San Francisco Chronicle* printed a photograph of Whitney with the matron of the San Francisco county jail under the headline, "Trying to Be Martyr" and subtitled, "Checking In for 300-Day Stay That Ended in Few Hours."

Whitney was the chairman of the California Communist Party from 1936 to 1944, which made her one of the few Communist Party women in a leadership role. She did not run for election in California after 1940, when she got almost 100,000 votes in her campaign for the U.S. Senate, because that year the state passed a law keeping the Communist Party off the ballot. She had been in an automobile accident during the 1940 campaign and had broken a number of ribs, but insisted on continuing the campaign nonetheless.

Whitney also retained her belief that the American creed was one of liberty and equality and that she was simply following her ancestors' footsteps in insisting that free speech was a major part of liberty. She continued her speaking career through the 1940s, at various times agitating against the closing of a Communist bookstore and suing California local governments that refused to allow Communist Party meetings. She had long been involved in various antisegregation and minority farm workers' rights efforts, and she went on with those activities as well. According to her biographer, one result was a number of Latina and African American children in California named Anita.

Before the Japanese attacked Pearl Harbor in 1941 and the United States entered World War II, Whitney was one of the people at a Communist Party national committee meeting that endorsed American involvement in a war against Hitler. After the attack, the 75-year-old Whitney tried to register for civilian defense but was told she was too old for the job. Instead, she wound surgical bandages twice a week for the Red Cross and opened her home to meetings about air raid precautions. In 1942 she was arrested in Sacramento for speaking at a public meeting held without a permit. Her speech exhorted the small crowd to vote for state Democrats. The Communist Party was still banned from the ballot, and she favored the Democrats because their party was committed to pursuing the war against Germany. The Communist Party disbanded in 1944 as a sign of its support for the allies in World War II, reconstituting itself as the Communist Political Association. Whitney became the vice president of the California branch.

Whitney was no more inclined to let age keep her from causes she espoused than she would permit the government to do so. In the early 1950s, when she was in her 80s, she participated in the short-lived Negro Labor Council's antisegregation sit-ins. A colleague remembered the 83-year-old Whitney being carried to a longshoreman's rally and speaking against the convictions of radicals under the Smith Act, which outlawed the kind of advocacy that had resulted in Whitney's arrest for criminal syndicalism. She remained a member of the Communist Party's national committee in those years, when the House Committee on Un-American Activities and Senator Joseph McCarthy were trampling Americans' rights of speech and association. She had lived through the first Red Scare, during the post–World War I years; now she lived through another. She was undaunted. "We've simply got to fight harder than ever now," she had told the Communist newspaper *People's World* in 1947. "You grow through struggle."

Charlotte Anita Whitney died in 1955, at age 87. She had been ill and out of the public eye for a year. Her lawyer estimated her estate, including the San Francisco house she had moved into some years earlier, as worth somewhere between $20,000 and $30,000. It was hardly the more substantial amount she was heir to before she began giving her money to what she considered to be good causes. Whitney left her estate to a nephew, presumably the one who had paid her fine. She was buried with her parents in Oakland, but she had been such a controversial figure that no headstone was placed on her grave.

The ACLU's campaign for free speech and against criminal syndicalism laws had not ended with Anita Whitney's case. In 1925, the organization's California branch received a $5,000 loan from the Garland Fund to examine the use of the California statute. It hired George W. Kirchwey, a criminologist, to carry out the work. Kirchwey's history included stints as a dean of the Albany Law School and Columbia University's law school, warden of Sing Sing, and director of the American Society of International Law. In 1926 the ACLU published the resultant forty-seven-page "A Survey of the Workings of the Criminal Syndicalism Law in California." Unsurprisingly, it was critical of the law, noting the "curious situation" that in California "a man may advocate [but not incite] burglary or robbery or murder . . . or any unlawful methods of terrorism without fear of the law so long as his advocacy does not aim at the accomplishment 'of a change in industrial ownership or control' or of 'any political change.'" There had been over 531 indictments since the act took effect in April 1919 but, as in Whitney's case, not one of the indictments mentioned specific acts of which those named were allegedly guilty. Five hundred and four of those indicted were apprehended, and 292 of the indictments had been dismissed without trial. Of the 264 persons tried, 164 were convicted; 55 of the 114 appeals that followed were successful. The only organizations whose members were prosecuted were the Communist Labor Party and the I.W.W., and almost all of those convicted were found guilty only of membership but not of other actions. The norms of due process were routinely ignored in the trials, as they had been in Whitney's case.

By 1926, Kirchwey noted, "the attitude and temper of the public" had changed and the law was no longer being used. Historian Woodrow Whitten reported some years later that there were no arrests under the act from August 1923 through 1930 (the law was utilized later in the 1930s, however, to prosecute unionizing farm workers). The organizations that had seemed so fearsome in the postwar years were no longer perceived as such. The criminal syndicalism law nonetheless remained on the books, as repeated efforts throughout the 1930s by the ACLU and other organizations to have it repealed had no success in the California legislature. The Supreme Court's holding in *Brandenburg v. Ohio*, however, effectively rendered criminal syndicalism laws unconstitutional as applied to mere membership or advocacy. The California statute was specifically declared unconstitutional by a state district court of appeal in 1971. It was formally removed from the statute books in 1991, with the legislature adding in what seems to have been a lighthearted moment, "The Legislature finds and declares that every person has the right to speak out, to poke fun, and to stir up controversy without fear of criminal prosecution."

"My life for the most part has been uneventful and quite the ordinary life of a woman born in the middle class," Whitney wrote at the beginning of 1926, before the Supreme Court decided to rehear her case. "It does happen that I was caught in a whirl of a stream," she acknowledged, but that was only because "I was made a rebel against the existing order by the very logic of events." It may seem hard to believe that Whitney considered that a privileged woman involving herself in public life early in the twentieth century and becoming a "rebel" was quite ordinary. She was adamant, however, that she did no more than follow the ideals of her forefathers and the constitutional philosophy they laid down for the United States.

That philosophy was equally important to Louis Dembitz Brandeis. Both he and Whitney worked from within to reform the American economic system, although in quite different ways: he, during his pre-Court years as a *pro bono* attorney and political activist; she, following her unwavering belief that party activism and the kind of public speech for which she believed her ancestors had fought would produce a just society. They were alike in their certainty that the American people, when sufficiently informed, would opt to do the right thing. Education was the key, and education depended on free speech.

Whitney liked to quote Thomas Jefferson, and the particular words she would sometimes cite can perhaps be viewed as the first American statement of the incitement test as the only legitimate criterion if speech is to be proscribed. Jefferson wrote in the Act for Establishing Religious Freedom that "it is time enough for the rightful purposes of civil government, for its officers to interfere when principles break out into overt acts against peace and good order." Free speech became something of a mantra for Anita Whitney and, as well, for Louis Dembitz Brandeis. In their very different ways they played a major role in creating the speech jurisprudence that is now one of the hallmarks of the American political system. One can only imagine that they would both be pleased.

CASES AND STATUTES CITED

Cases

Abrams v. United States, 250 U.S. 616 (1919)

Barron v. Baltimore, 32 U.S. (7 Pet.) 243 (1833)

Bartnicki v. Vopper, 532 U.S. 514 (2001)

Brandenburg v. Ohio, 395 U.S. 444 (1969)

Brown v. Board of Education, 347 U.S. 483 (1954)

Buckley v. Valeo, 424 U.S. 1 (1976)

Canada (Human Rights Comm.) v. Taylor (1990), Judgments of the Supreme Court of Canada, 13 C.H.R.R. D/435 (S.C.C.)

Citizens United v. Federal Election Commission, 558 U.S. 310 (2010)

Cohen v. California, 403 U.S. 15 (1971)

Collin v. Smith (the Skokie case), 447 F.Supp. 676 (N.D. Ill., 1977); 578 F.2d 1197 (7th Cir., 1978)

Debs v. United States, 249 U.S. 211 (1919)

De Jonge v. Oregon, 299 U.S. 353 (1937)

Dennis v. United States, 341 U.S. 494 (1951)

Frohwerk v. United States, 249 U.S. 204 (1919)

Gilbert v. Minnesota, 254 U.S. 325 (1920)

Gitlow v. New York, 268 U.S. 652 (1925)

Holder v. Humanitarian Law Project, 561 U.S. 1 (2010)

Marbury v. Madison, 5 U.S. (1 Cranch) 137 (1803)

Masses Publishing Co. v. Patten, 244 Fed. 535 (S.D.N.Y. 1917), 246 F. 24 (2d Cir., 1917)

McCutcheon v. FEC, 134 S.Ct. 1434 (2014)

McDonald v. City of Chicago, 561 U.S. 742 (2010)

Milwaukee Social Democratic Publishing Co. v. Burleson, 255 U.S. 407 (1921)

Muller v. Oregon, 208 U.S. 412 (1908)

Near v. Minnesota, 283 U.S. 697 (1931)

New York Times *v. Sullivan,* 376 U.S. 254 (1964)

Patterson v. Colorado, 205 U.S. 454 (1907)

People v. Ruthenberg, 229 Mich. 315, 201 N.W. 358 (1924)

People v. Whitney, 57 Cal. App. 449, 207 P. 698 (1922)

Pierce v. United States, 252 U.S. 239 (1920)

Planned Parenthood of Southeastern Pennsylvania v. Casey, 505 U.S. 833 (1992)

Powell v. Alabama, 287 U.S. 45 (1932)

Reno v. ACLU, 521 U.S. 844 (1997)

Schaefer v. United States, 251 U.S. 466 (1920)

Schenck v. United States, 249 U.S. 47 (1919)

Schneiderman v. United States, 320 U.S. 118 (1943)

Stromberg v. California, 283 U.S. 359 (1931)

Taylor and Western Guard Party v. Canada, Communication No. 104/1981, Report of the Human Rights Committee, 38 U.N. GAOR, Supp. No. 40 (A/38/40) 231 (1983), para. 8(b), decision reported in part at (1983), 5 C.H.R.R. D/2097

Texas v. Johnson, 491 U.S. 397 (1989)

United States v. Alvarez, 132 S.Ct. 2537 (2012)

United States v. Carolene Products Co., 304 U.S. 144 (1938)

United States v. National Treasury Employees Union, 513 U.S. 454 (1995)

Whitney v. California, 269 U.S. 538 (1925), 274 U.S. 357 (1927)

Yates v. United States, 354 U.S. 298 (1957)

Statutes

California syndicalism law: West's Ann. Cal. Penal Code §§ 11400 to 11402; repealed by Stats. 1991, ch. 186 (A.B.436), § 10.

Espionage Act of 1917, Pub.L. 65-24; ch. 30, 40 Stat. 217

Sedition Act of 1918, Pub.L. 65-150; ch. 75, 40 Stat. 553

Selective Draft Act (Selective Service Act) of 1917, Pub.L. 65-12; ch. 15, 40 Stat. 76

Trading with the Enemy Act of 1917, Pub.L. 65-91; ch. 106, 40 Stat. 411

November 13, 1856   Louis Dembitz Brandeis born in Louisville, Kentucky

July 7, 1867   Charlotte Anita Whitney born in San Francisco, California

1875–1878   Brandeis earns bachelor's and master's degrees from Harvard Law School

1879–1916   Brandeis practices law in Boston; involved in public interest law from 1900 on

1885   Whitney enters Wellesley College; graduates in 1889

1890   Publication of Samuel D. Warren and Louis D. Brandeis, "The Right to Privacy," in the *Harvard Law Review*

1893   Whitney visits and begins working at College Settlement House, New York City

1901–1907   Whitney serves as secretary of Associated Charities; begins lobbying for woman suffrage in California

1903   Whitney becomes Alameda County's first juvenile probation officer

1905   Industrial Workers of the World (I.W.W.) organized in Chicago, Illinois

1909–1912   I.W.W. "free speech fights"

1911–1914   Whitney involved in suffrage efforts in Californa, Oregon, Nevada, and as an officer of the National American Woman Suffrage Association; helps organize and becomes president of the California Civic League; works with the Society for the Abolition of the Death Penalty in California; lobbies in Sacramento for public causes such as women's right to sit on juries and minimum wages for women and children.

1912   I.W.W. textile workers' strike in Lawrence, Massachusetts

1913   I.W.W. textile workers' strike in Patterson, New Jersey

August 3, 1913   Wheatland Hops "Riot"

1914   Whitney joins the Socialist Party of America

1916   Brandeis appointed to the U.S. Supreme Court

1919   Emergency National Convention of the National

	Socialist Party; creation of Communist Labor Party and Communist Party
1919	U.S. Supreme Court upholds convictions for antiwar speech in *Schenck v. U.S.* (March 3), *Frohwerk v. United States* (March 10), *Debs v. United States* (March 10)
April 30, 1919	California criminal syndicalism law enacted; takes immediate effect
June 1919	Zechariah Chafee's "Freedom of Speech in War Time" published in the *Harvard Law Review*
November 9, 1919	Founding convention of the California Communist Labor Party
November 10, 1919	Supreme Court upholds convictions in *Abrams v. United States*, with Justice Holmes writing a dissent for himself and Justice Brandeis
November 28, 1919	Whitney arrested and charged with criminal syndicalism
January 20, 1920	Roger Baldwin, Crystal Eastman, and colleagues create the American Civil Liberties Union
January 27, 1920	Whitney trial begins; continues through February 20
February 7, 1920	Death of Whitney attorney Thomas M. O'Connor
February 20, 1920	Whitney convicted of criminal syndicalism
March 1920	Supreme Court decides *Schaefer v. United States* and *Pierce v. United States*, with Justice Brandeis writing dissents for himself and Justice Holmes
December 13, 1920	Supreme Court upholds advocacy conviction in *Gilbert v. Minnesota*, with Justice Brandeis dissenting
April 25, 1922	California District Court of Appeal upholds Whitney's conviction
1922	Whitney's lawyers petition the California Supreme Court for a hearing; the court declines to hear the case
May 2, 1923	Charles Ruthenberg convicted of criminal syndicalism in Michigan
June 8, 1925	U.S. Supreme Court upholds criminal anarchy conviction in *Gitlow v. New York*, with Justices Holmes and Brandeis dissenting, but says that the First Amendment's speech and press clauses are binding on the states
October 6, 1925	Supreme Court hears oral argument in *Whitney v. California*

October 19, 1925	Supreme Court announces it will not decide the *Whitney* case
December 14, 1925	Supreme Court agrees to rehear the case
March 18, 1926	Supreme Court rehears oral argument in *Whitney*
March 2, 1927	Charles Ruthenberg dies, mooting case of *Ruthenberg v. Michigan*
May 16, 1927	Supreme Court upholds Whitney's conviction, with Justice Brandeis writing a concurrence for himself and Justice Holmes
June 20, 1927	California Governor C. C. Young pardons Whitney
1928	Whitney runs for U.S. Senate on Communist Party ticket
1929	Whitney arrested at Communist Party demonstrations
January 30, 1931	Supreme Court hears oral argument in the case of *Near v. Minnesota*, with Justice Brandeis commenting on the importance of a free press
1932	Whitney moves from Oakland to San Francisco
1934	Whitney runs for California state controller and receives 100,820 votes; convicted for falsely certifying signatures on election petition
1936–1944	Whitney serves as chairman of the California Communist Party
1938	Whitney runs for California state controller
1940	Whitney runs for U.S. Senate
October 5, 1941	Death of Louis D. Brandeis
December 1941	Whitney turned down as participant in World War II civilian defense efforts because of age; volunteers for American Red Cross instead
1942	Whitney arrested for speaking at public meeting without a permit
1950s	Whitney participates in antisegregation and farm workers' demonstrations
February 4, 1955	Death of Anita Whitney
June 9, 1969	U.S. Supreme Court decides *Brandenburg v. Ohio*, overturning *Whitney v. California*

BIBLIOGRAPHICAL ESSAY

Note from the Series Editors: The following bibliographical essay contains the major pri-
mary and secondary sources the author consulted for this volume. We have asked all
authors in the series to omit formal citations in order to make our volumes more readable,
inexpensive, and appealing for students and general readers. In adopting this format,
Landmark Law Cases and American Society follows the precedent of a number of highly
regarded and widely consulted series.

Anita Whitney

Anita Whitney's papers were destroyed or have been lost. Her articles about
her life before the final Supreme Court decision in her case were published
as "My Story" by the *San Francisco Daily News* of January 14–25, 1926. A copy
is available at the Oakland Free Library in California. Part of the series was
later serialized in the *Pittsburgh Press.* "My Story," February 15, 1926, 19; February 16, 1926, 7. Her article recounting her experience in jail is Charlotte Anita
Whitney, "The Alameda County Jail," in the *Survey* of December 25, 1920,
452–453, 470.

Al Richmond, one of Whitney's colleagues, had access to her files and in-
terviewed her for a biography designed to commemorate her 75th birthday.
The result is, unsurprisingly, something of a hagiography, but judging from
the articles in the newspapers listed above and below, it recounts key events
in her life accurately. Al Richmond, *Native Daughter: The Story of Anita Whitney*
(San Francisco: Anita Whitney 75th Anniversary Committee, 1942), available
at http://archive.org/stream/nativedaughterstoorichrich/nativedaughterstoo
richrich_djvu.txt. Lisa Rubens, "The Patrician Radical Charlotte Anita Whitney," *65 California History* 158 (September 1986) is a good short biographical
account whose author had the benefit of interviews with people who knew
Whitney.

Frederick Clifton Pierce, *The Descendants of John Whitney, Who Came from*
London, England, to Watertown, Massachusetts, in 1635 (Chicago: 1895), 412, has information about Whitney's ancestors, as does the Whitney Research Group,
http://whitneygen.org/wrg/index.php/Archive:Charlotte_Anita_Whitney_
(1867–1955). Follow the footnotes for data about specific ancestors. Other
sources for the family's early involvement in the Massachusetts Bay Colony
and Harvard College are Jacob Bailey Moore, *Lives of the Governors of New Plym-*
outh, and Massachusetts Bay (Boston: C. D. Strong, 1851), 287, 289–290, available at
http://babel.hathitrust.org/cgi/pt?id=nyp.33433081781225;view=1up;seq=11 and
http://books.google.com/books?id=ossDAAAAYAAJ&pg=PA273#v=one

page&q&f=false; *Harvard Library Bulletin* 29 (April 1981), 365; Mason Hammond, "A Harvard Armory: Part II," *Harvard Library Bulletin* 1, no. 3 (Autumn 1947): 361–402, 365–369, accessible at http://pds.lib.harvard.edu/pds/view /2573358?n=14334; and Commonwealth of Massachusetts, "Joseph Dudley (1647–1720)," http://www.mass.gov/portal/government-taxes/laws/interactive-state-house/historical/governors-of-massachusetts/province-of-new-england-1686-1692/joseph-dudley-1647-1720.html. Justice Stephen Field's will is reproduced in John C. Hogan and Ewald W. Schnitzer, "The Last Will and Testament of Stephen J. Field," 36 *California Historical Society Quarterly* 41 (1957), 50–52.

Whitney's experience at Wellesley was similar to that of other women in colleges and universities in the late 1880s. Mabel Newcomer, *A Century of Higher Education for American Women* (New York: Harper & Brothers, 1959), and Barbara Miller Solomon, *In the Company of Educated Women: A History of Women and Higher Education in America* (New Haven, CT: Yale University Press, 1985) are among the good sources on women and higher education during those years.

While not specifically about the College Settlement House in New York City at which Whitney worked, there are numerous works devoted to the history of settlement houses in general. The information about them in chapter 1 comes from John P. Rousmaniere, "Cultural Hybrid in the Slums: The College Woman and the Settlement House, 1889–1894," 22 *American Quarterly* 45 (Spring, 1970), 46; Judith Ann Trolander, *Professionalism and Social Change: From the Settlement House Movement to Neighborhood Centers, 1886 to the Present* (New York: Columbia University Press, 1987), 10–12; Sarah Henry Lederman, "Settlement Houses in the United States" (American Jewish Historical Society), at http://jwa.org/encyclopedia/article/settlement-houses-in-united-states); Brigid O'Farrell, *She Was One of Us: Eleanor Roosevelt and the American Worker* (Ithaca, NY: Cornell University Press, 2010), 7–8; and Blanche Wiesen Cook, *Eleanor Roosevelt*, vol. 1, *1884–1933* (New York: Viking, 1992), 135, 137–138.

Much of Whitney's public life from the time she returned to her parents' home in Oakland is documented in California newspapers, including the *Los Angeles Times, Los Angeles Herald, San Francisco Chronicle, Oakland Tribune,* and *San Francisco Call,* as well as in "My Story," mentioned above. I have relied heavily upon them for her history. Some, like the *San Francisco Daily News,* appear to be archived only in California libraries, but articles from the *Los Angeles Times* and *San Francisco Chronicle* can be found in databases such as ProQuest. The *Oakland Tribune* is archived on two commercial websites: www .newspaperarchive.com and www.newspapers.com. WorldCat (www.worldcat .org) lists collections at public libraries. Articles from the *San Francisco Call* can be accessed from the Library of Congress's *Chronicling America* (1836–1922) and from the California Digital Newspaper Collection, http://cdnc.ucr.edu /cgi-bin/cdnc.

Selina Solomons, *How We Won the Vote in California: A True Story of the Campaign of 1911* (San Francisco: New Woman Publishing Company, 1912), and Robert P. J. Cooney Jr., "California Women Suffrage Centennial: A Brief Summary of the 1911 Campaign," http://www.sos.ca.gov/elections/suffrage /history/, tell some of the story of Whitney's involvement in the suffrage movement in that state. Holly J. McCammon, *The U.S. Women's Jury Movements and Strategic Adaptation: A More Just Verdict* (Cambridge: Cambridge University Press, 2012), 56–59, recounts the effort in which Whitney was involved to secure women's right to serve on juries. The results of Whitney's election campaigns can be found at JoinCalifornia, www.joincalifornia.com.

Labor History

Eric Arnesen, ed., *Encyclopedia of U.S. Labor and Working-Class History*, 3 vols. (New York: Routledge, 2007) is a very good place to start an examination of American labor history.

The I.W.W. is the focus of Melvyn Dubofsky, *We Shall Be All: A History of the Industrial Workers of the World*. It was published by Quadrangle in 1967 but most readers will prefer a shorter edition, edited by Joseph A. McCartin (Champaign: University of Illinois Press, 2000). There are a number of other solid works about the Wobblies, including Eric Thomas Chester, *Wobblies in Their Heyday: The Rise and Destruction of the Industrial Workers of the World during the World War I Era* (Santa Barbara, CA: Praeger, 2014); Joseph Robert Conlin, *Bread and Roses Too: Studies of the Wobblies* (Santa Barbara, CA: Greenwood Publishing Corp., 1969); and Patrick Renshaw, *The Wobblies: The Story of the IWW and Syndicalism in the United States* (New York: Doubleday & Co., 1967). Philip S. Foner, *History of the Labor Movement in the United States*, vol. 4 (New York: International Publishers, 1965) is devoted to the Wobblies.

Bruce Watson, *Bread and Roses: Mills, Migrants, and the Struggle for the American Dream* (New York: Viking, 2005) is about the Lawrence, Massachusetts, strike, as is William Cahn, *1912: The Bread & Roses Strike* (Cleveland, OH: Pilgrim Press, 1980). The Ray Stannard Baker article quoted in chapter 1 is "Lawrence Textile Strike," *American Magazine*, May 1912, 19–30. There is also a Bread and Roses Centennial Exhibit at http://exhibit.breadandrosescentennial.org/.

After having receded from the public eye, the Wobblies have recently had something of a comeback. "Here Come the Wobblies!," *Sacramento News & Review*, January 13, 2005, available at http://www.newsreview.com/sacramento /here-come-the-wobblies/content?oid=33285. The organization maintains a website, www.iww.org, that includes material such as a history, minutes of the founding convention, and sketches of leading Wobblies.

For the Wobblies' free speech fights, see David Rabban, "The IWW Free Speech Fights and Popular Concepts of Free Speech before World War I," 80

Virginia Law Review 1055 (August 1994), which is an authoritative overview of the fights and their importance for the development of American attitudes toward speech, and Rosalie Shanks, "The I.W.W. Free Speech Movement: San Diego, 1912," 19 *Journal of San Diego History* (Winter 1973), available at http://www.sandiegohistory.org/journal/73winter/speech.htm. Harris Weinstock, *A Report to His Excellency Hiram W. Johnson, Governor of California, as Commissioner Appointed on April 15, 1912, to Investigate Charges of Cruelty and All Matters Pertaining to the Recent Disturbances in the City of San Diego and the County of San Diego* (Sacramento, CA: State Printing Office, 1912) is the official report about the speech riots in San Diego.

Ray Ginger, *The Bending Cross: A Biography of Eugene Victor Debs* (New Brunswick, NJ: Rutgers University Press, 1947) and Ernest Freeberg, *Democracy's Prisoner: Eugene V. Debs, the Great War, and the Right to Dissent* (Cambridge, MA: Harvard University Press, 2008) are both useful works about that Wobbly leader. The Canton speech that landed Debs in jail is at http://debsfoundation.org/pdf/canton-and-court.pdf.

Kevin Starr, *Endangered Dreams: the Great Depression in California* (Oxford: Oxford University Press, 1996); Carey McWilliams, *Factories in the Field: The Story of Migratory Farm Labor in California* (New York: Little, Brown and Co., 1939; Berkeley: University of California Press, 2000); and Cletus E. Daniel, *Bitter Harvest: A History of California Farmworkers, 1870–1941* (Ithaca, NY: Cornell University Press, 1981) are fine studies of agricultural workers in the Southwest during the years relevant to Anita Whitney. Chapter 9 of the McWilliams volume puts the Wheatland "riot" in the context of the free speech fights and Wobbly history generally. Woodrow C. Whitten, "The Wheatland Episode," 17 *Pacific Historical Review* 37 (February 1948), tells the story of the event, as does "Commission of Immigration and Housing of California, Report to the Governor of California," reprinted in Carleton H. Parker, *The Casual Laborer and Other Essays* (San Diego, CA: Harcourt, Brace and Howe, 1920), 171–199. Parker was the author of the commission's report. George L. Bell, "The Wheatlands Hops-Fields' Riot," *Outlook*, May 16, 1914, 118–123, is another contemporary account. There are pictures of the Wheatland camp at https://play.google.com/books/reader?id=kJpQAAAAYAAJ&printsec=frontcover&output=reader&hl=en_US&pg=GBS.PA20. Clemens P. Work, *Darkest before Dawn: Sedition and Free Speech in the American West* (Albuquerque: University of New Mexico Press, 2005) details the close relationship between fear of the Wobblies and sedition prosecutions in the West, with the emphasis on Montana. Its sedition statute was a model for the federal one.

The Socialist and Communist Labor Parties

David A. Shannon, *The Socialist Party of America: A History* (New York: Mac-millan Co., 1955); John H. M. Laslett and Seymour Martin Lipset, *Failure of a Dream? Essays in the History of American Socialism*, rev. ed. (Berkeley: University of California Press, 1984); and James Weinstein, *The Decline of Socialism in America, 1912–1925* (New York: Vintage Books, 1969) are all solid histories of the party. Shannon is also the author of "The Socialist Party before the First World War: An Analysis," 38 *Mississippi Valley Historical Review* 279 (September 1951). The Socialist Party platform of 1912, very like that of 1914 when Whitney joined, is at http://www.sageamericanhistory.net/progressive/docs/Socialist-Plat1912.htm.

Ralph E. Shaffer, "Formation of the California Communist Labor Party," 36 *Pacific Historical Review* 59 (February 1967) covers the Socialist Party as well as the creation of the CLP. The same author's "Communism in California, 1919–1924: 'Orders from Moscow' or Independent Western Radicalism?," 34 *Science & Society* 412 (Winter 1970) also provides useful history. Chapter 11 of Theodore Draper's encyclopedic *The Roots of American Communism* (New York: Viking, 1957; New Brunswick, NJ: Transaction Publishers, 2003) is about the 1919 Socialist Party split that resulted in creation of the Communist Labor Party. It is available online at https://libcom.org/files/Theodore%20Draper%20The%20Roots%20of%20American%20Communism%20%20 2003.pdf. There is a website devoted to the history of the CLP, with links to various documents, including the minutes of the founding convention (http://www.marxists.org/history/usa/eam/cpa/communistparty.html) and the party's constitution (http://www.marxisthistory.org/history/usa/parties/cpusa/1919/0905-clp-constitution.pdf).

Rose Pastor Stokes wrote about her experiences in the Socialist Party in *"I Belong to the Working Class": The Unfinished Autobiography of Rose Pastor Stokes*, ed. Herbert Shapiro and David L. Sterling (Athens: University of Georgia Press, 1992). Arthur Zipser and Pearl Zipser, *Fire and Grace: The Life of Rose Pastor Stokes* (Athens: University of Georgia Press, 1989) is a biography.

Civil Liberties during World War I and the Following Years

Paul L. Murphy, *World War I and the Origin of Civil Liberties in the United States* (New York: W. W. Norton & Co., 1979) provides scholarly coverage of that era. Robert K. Murray, *Red Scare: A Study in National Hysteria, 1919–1920* (Westport, CT: Greenwood Press, 1955) is a more popular version of the events, as its sub-title suggests. The era is also covered in chapter 2 of Samuel Walker, *Presidents and Civil Liberties from Wilson to Obama: A Story of Poor Custodians* (Cambridge: Cambridge University Press, 2012); Arthur H. Garrison, *Supreme Court Juris-*

prudence in Times of National Crisis, Terrorism and War: A Historical Perspective (Lanham, MD: Lexington Books, 2011), chapter 3; and chapter 3 of Geoffrey R. Stone, *Perilous Times: Free Speech in Wartime from the Sedition Act of 1798 to the War on Terrorism* (New York: W. W. Norton & Co., 2004). The Stone book as a whole provides a wonderful panoramic view of war and speech as well as other civil liberties throughout American history.

The Espionage and Sedition Acts and the persecution of people opposed to World War I are detailed in H. C. Peterson and Gilbert C. Fite, *Opponents of War, 1917–1918* (Madison: University of Wisconsin Press, 1957) and William Preston, *Aliens and Dissenters: Federal Suppression of Radicals, 1903–1933* (Champaign: University of Illinois Press, 1994). Geoffrey R. Stone, "Judge Learned Hand and the Espionage Act of 1917: A Mystery Unraveled," 70 *University of Chicago Law Review* 335 (Winter 2003) includes a discussion of congressional debates while the Espionage Act was being considered and argues that the courts subsequently gave the act a far more repressive interpretation than the legislators intended. Thomas A. Lawrence, "Eclipse of Liberty: Civil Liberties in the United States during the First World War," 21 *Wayne Law Review* 33 (1974–1975) contends that the judiciary, the executive branch, and much of the legal profession suffered from the same hysteria that afflicted the citizenry. The article includes biographical information about the Supreme Court justices at the time of the 1919 speech cases.

The report by Frankfurter, Chafee, and other law professors on the Justice Department's civil liberties violations is R. G. Brown, Zechariah Chafee Jr., Felix Frankfurter, et al., *Report upon the Illegal Practices of the United States Department of Justice* (Washington, DC: National Popular Government League, 1920), accessible at http://www.forgottenbooks.org/readbook/To_the_American _People_1920_1000540114#1.

For a description of the factors that were responsible for much of the repression, see Ann Hagedorn, *Savage Peace: Hope and Fear in America, 1919* (New York: Simon & Schuster, 2007). Anthony Read, *The World on Fire: 1919 and the Battle with Bolshevism* (New York: W. W. Norton, 2008) covers some of the same ground. The psychological effects of the Boston police strike are recounted in Francis Russell, *A City in Terror: Calvin Coolidge and the 1919 Boston Police Strike* (Boston, MA: Beacon Press, 1975).

Speech and the First Amendment

Three of the now-classic works on the First Amendment are Thomas Emerson, *The System of Freedom of Expression* (New York: Random House, 1970); Lee C. Bollinger, *The Tolerant Society: Freedom of Speech and Extremist Speech in America* (Oxford: Oxford University Press, 1986); and Harry Kalven, *A Worthy Tradition: Freedom of Speech in America* (New York: Harper & Row, 1988).

Anthony Lewis, *Freedom for the Thought That We Hate: A Biography of the First Amendment* (New York: Basic Books, 2007) is a wonderfully written and highly accessible account, by the *New York Times'* first Supreme Court reporter, of the development of and rationale for free speech and press. There is a debate about exactly what the framers of the First Amendment meant in David A. Anderson, "The Origins of the Press Clause," 30 *UCLA Law Review* 455 (1983) and Leonard W. Levy, *Legacy of Suppression* (Cambridge, MA: Harvard University Press, 1960) and *Emergence of a Free Press* (Lanham, MD: Ivan R. Dee, 1985).

The development of free speech jurisprudence in the first decades of the twentieth century is detailed at length in David M. Rabban, "The Emergence of Modern First Amendment Doctrine," 50 *University of Chicago Law Review* 1205 (Fall 1983) and G. Edward White, "The First Amendment Comes of Age: The Emergence of Free Speech in Twentieth-Century America," 95 *Michigan Law Review* 299 (November 1996). Rabban covers the pre–World War I Free Speech League as well as the early years of the ACLU in three works: "The Free Speech League, the ACLU, and Changing Conceptions of Free Speech in American History," 45 *Stanford Law Review* 47 (November 1992); *The First Amendment in Its Forgotten Years*, 90 *Yale Law Journal* 514 (1981); and the longer *Free Speech in its Forgotten Years* (Cambridge: Cambridge University Press, 1997), which draws on the earlier articles.

There are well-written and very accessible books on two of the cases that preceded *Whitney*. Richard Polenberg, *Fighting Faiths: The Abrams Case, the Supreme Court, and Free Speech* (New York: Viking, 1987) and Marc Lendler, *Gitlow v. New York: Every Idea an Incitement* (Lawrence: University Press of Kansas, 2012). Benjamin Gitlow's own thoughts about his case are in *I Confess: the Truth about American Communism* (New York: E. P. Dutton & Co., 1940), 69, 71. Michael Hannon, *The People v. Benjamin Gitlow (1920)* (University of Minnesota Law Library, http://darrow.law.umn.edu/trialpdfs/Gitlow_Case.pdf) is a good account of the New York trial. The *New York Times* of December 1925 has a number of articles about Gitlow after he was freed. Fred W. Friendly, *Minnesota Rag: The Dramatic Story of the Landmark Supreme Court Case That Gave New Meaning to Freedom of the Press* (New York: Random House, 1981), tells the story of *Near v. Minnesota*, the case in which Brandeis spoke at oral argument about the need for a free press. Some of his remarks are quoted on 130–131.

The Alan Dershowitz quote in chapter 6 comes from Dershowitz, *Taking the Stand: My Life in the Law* (New York: Crown Publishers, 2013), 107.

Oliver Wendell Holmes Jr.

There are whole bookshelves filled with volumes about Justice Holmes, and I apologize to the authors of the many that cannot be listed here. A good place to begin for biographical information might be G. Edward White, *Oli-*

ver Wendell Holmes: Sage of the Supreme Court (Oxford: Oxford University Press, 2000) or Sheldon M. Novick, *Honorable Justice: The Life of Oliver Wendell Holmes* (New York: Little, Brown & Co., 1989). Holmes's own words are in Max Lerner, ed., *The Mind and Faith of Justice Holmes: His Speeches, Essays, Letters and Judicial Opinions* (Boston: Little, Brown and Company, 1945) and Ronald K. L. Collins, *The Fundamental Holmes: A Free Speech Chronicle and Reader* (Cambridge: Cambridge University Press, 2010). The Collins volume has extensive commentary as well as a collection of Holmes's opinions and other writings. Those interested in *Whitney* might see especially parts 5 and 6, as well as H. L. Pohlman, *Justice Oliver Wendell Holmes: Free Speech and the Living Constitution* (New York: New York University Press, 1991). Albert W. Alschuler, *Law without Values: The Life, Work, and Legacy of Justice Holmes* (Chicago, IL: University of Chicago Press, 2000), is one of the few accounts that is extremely critical of Holmes, portraying him as lacking in basic values.

For an extensive discussion of the influences on Holmes as he rethought his approach to speech, see G. Edward White, "Justice Holmes and the Modernization of Free Speech Jurisprudence: The Human Dimension," 80 *California Law Review* 391 (1992). Most scholars, including those listed here, have pointed to the marked change in Holmes's views. A dissenting voice, arguing that his views were consistent, can be found in Sheldon M. Novick, "The Unrevised Holmes and Freedom of Expression," 1991 *Supreme Court Review* 303 (1991). Thomas Healy, *The Great Dissent: How Oliver Wendell Holmes Changed His Mind—and Changed the History of Free Speech in America* (New York: Henry Holt and Co., 2013) also discusses Holmes's changed view of speech, although it minimizes Brandeis's contribution and barely mentions the *Whitney* case. The Ernest Freund article that took Holmes aback was "The Debs Case and Freedom of Speech" in the *New Republic* of May 3, 1919, 13–15.

The letters between Zechariah Chafee and Learned Hand, and between Holmes and Hand, are reproduced and discussed in Gerald Gunther, "Learned Hand and the Origins of Modern First Amendment Doctrine: Some Fragments of History," 27 *Stanford Law Review* 719 (1974–1975). Hand's opinion in the *Masses* case is covered in Vincent Blasi, "Learned Hand and the Self-Government Theory of the First Amendment: Masses Publishing Co. v. Patten," 61 *University of Colorado Law Review* 1 (1990).

Fred D. Ragan, "Justice Oliver Wendell Holmes, Jr., Zechariah Chafee, Jr., and the Clear and Present Danger Test for Free Speech: The First Year, 1919," 58 *Journal of American History* 24 (June 1971), examines the early Espionage Act cases and the influence of Chafee on Holmes. Chafee's "Freedom of Speech" was published in the *New Republic* of November 16, 1918, at 67. His "Freedom of Speech in War Time," 32 *Harvard Law Review* 932 (1919), can be found at https://archive.org/details/freedomspeechinoochafgoog. Chafee's *Free Speech in the United States* was first published by Harcourt, Brace and Howe in 1920, but that edition can be difficult to find. Harvard University Press printed an updated and expanded edition in 1941 and reprinted that edition subsequently. Donald L. Smith, *Zechariah Chafee, Jr., Defender of Liberty and Law* (Cambridge, MA: Harvard University Press, 1986) provides biographical information and discusses the evolution of Chafee's thinking about speech.

Samuel J. Konefsky, *The Legacy of Holmes and Brandeis: A Study in the Influence of Ideas* (New York: Macmillan Co., 1956), chs. 8 and 9, contains a useful comparison of the Holmes and Brandeis approaches to speech. Pnina Lahav, "Holmes and Brandeis: Libertarian and Republican Justifications for Free Speech," 4 *Journal of Law & Politics* 451 (1987–1988) examines the differing philosophies of the two justices.

An interesting side note: Vincent Blasi has pointed out that while the phrase "marketplace of ideas" is frequently attributed to Holmes, he never used it. His "competition of the market" was turned into "marketplace of ideas" by later commentators. Blasi, "Holmes and the Marketplace of Ideas," 2004 *Supreme Court Review* 1 (2004), at 14n41.

Louis Dembitz Brandeis

There are yet other whole bookshelves about Justice Brandeis. This author has an understandable preference for her own *Louis D. Brandeis: Justice for the People* (Cambridge, MA: Harvard University Press, 1984) and *Brandeis: Beyond Progressivism* (Lawrence: University of Kansas Press, 1993). Other useful biographies include Alpheus Thomas Mason, *Brandeis: A Free Man's Life* (New York: Viking Press, 1946) and Melvin I. Urofsky, *Louis D. Brandeis: A Life* (New York: Pantheon, 2009). While biographies of Brandeis are mostly admiring, Clyde Spillenger, "Elusive Advocate: Reconsidering Brandeis as People's Lawyer," 105 *Yale Law Journal* 1445 (1995–1996) presents a critical view of Brandeis as a lawyer, and Thomas K. McCraw, *Prophets of Regulation: Charles Francis Adams, Louis D. Brandeis, James M. Landis, and Alfred E. Kahn* (Cambridge, MA: Harvard University Press, 1984) criticizes his economic ideas.

Many of Brandeis's own words are reproduced in Philippa Strum, *Brandeis on Democracy* (Lawrence: University of Kansas Press, 1994), which is a compilation of some of Brandeis's speeches, judicial opinions, and other writings. His writings can also be found in *Business—A Profession* (Boston, MA: Small, Maynard, 1914); *The Curse of Bigness*, ed. Osmond K. Fraenkel (New York: Viking Press, 1934); and Alfred Lief, ed., *The Social and Economic Views of Mr. Justice Brandeis* (New York: Vanguard Press, 1930). Melvin I. Urofsky and David W. Levy are the editors of the five-volume *Letters of Louis D. Brandeis* (Albany: State University of New York Press, 1971–1978) and two other volumes of his letters: *"Half Brother, Half Son": The Letters of Louis D. Brandeis to Felix Frankfurter*

(Norman: University of Oklahoma Press, 1991) and *The Family Letters of Louis D. Brandeis* (Norman: University of Oklahoma Press, 2002).

Brandeis's comment about thinking "through" the meaning of free speech comes from the "Memorandum" written by Felix Frankfurter after conversations with Brandeis in 1922–1926 and is in the Brandeis Papers, Harvard Law School (Untitled Notebook, Box 114-7 and 114-8). Frankfurter's handwriting makes the original difficult to read. The Library of Congress has a typescript, reportedly put together by Alexander Bickel, which differs in some ways from the original. Frankfurter Papers, Library of Congress, Box 224. The memorandum is also in Melvin I. Urofsky, "The Brandeis-Frankfurter Conversations," 1985 *Supreme Court Review* 299 (1985). The conversation about speech, dated August 8, 1923, is at 323–324. The Brandeis article about privacy mentioned in chapter 7 is Samuel D. Warren and Louis D. Brandeis, "The Right to Privacy," 4 *Harvard Law Review* 193 (December 15, 1890).

The former Brandeis colleague and clerks quoted in chapter 6 are, respectively, Alvin Johnson, letter to Brandeis, November 11, 1936, quoted in Alexander Bickel, *The Unpublished Opinions of Mr. Justice Brandeis* (Cambridge, MA: Harvard University Press, 1957), 163; Donald Richberg, "The Industrial Liberalism of Mr. Justice Brandeis," 31 *Columbia Law Review* 1094 (November, 1931), at 1100; and David Riesman, "Notes for an Essay on Justice Brandeis," sent to Felix Frankfurter, May 22, 1936, in the Felix Frankfurter Papers at the Library of Congress, Box 127, 1–2. Jonathan Turley, "The 9 Greatest Supreme Court Justices," July 29, 2009, http://www.historynet.com/the-9-greatest-supreme-court-justices.htm; Cass R. Sunstein, "Home-Run Hitters of the Supreme Court," *Bloomberg View*, April 1, 2014, http://www.bloombergview.com /articles/2014-04-01/home-run-hitters-of-the-supreme-court; and Bruce Allen Murphy and Maria A. Fekete, "Louis Dembitz Brandeis," in *Great American Judges*, ed. John R. Vile (Santa Barbara, CA: ABC-Clio, 2003), 1:121–130, are typical assessments by scholars of Brandeis's importance.

Whitney v. California

The transcript of the Whitney trial was sent to the U.S. Supreme Court on appeal and is in the library of the Supreme Court. Record of Transcript, *Charlotte Anita Whitney, Plaintiff in Error vs. The People of the State of California*, Supreme Court of the United States, October Term 1925. Much of the transcript can also be found in Fund for the Republic, *Conspiracy Trials in America, 1919–1953* (Yonkers, NY: Michael Glazier, Inc., 1978), part 6. Haig Bosmajian, *Anita Whitney, Louis Brandeis, and the First Amendment* (Madison, NJ: Fairleigh Dickinson University Press, 2010) is a solid account of the case and its societal context. It includes an interesting chapter analyzing the language changes in the various drafts of the Brandeis concurrence. Woodrow Whitten, "The Trial of Charlotte Anita Whitney," 15 *Pacific Historical Review* 296 (September 1946) is a short account, written with the benefit of the trial transcript, to which some of the commentators who have written about the case apparently did not have access. Claire Shipman, "The Conviction of Anita Whitney," *Nation*, March 20, 1920 (365–367), and Anna Porter, "The Case of Anita Whitney," *New Republic*, July 6, 1921 (165–166), are accounts in Progressive magazines of that era. "The Jailing of Anita Whitney," in *Literary Digest* of November 14, 1925, 14–15, was written after the Supreme Court decided not to hear the case and is a reaction to its nondecision.

There are a number of fine scholarly articles about the case, with an emphasis on the Brandeis opinion. The one that should not be missed is Vincent Blasi, "The First Amendment and the Ideal of Civic Courage: The Brandeis Opinion in Whitney v. California," 29 *William and Mary Law Review* 658 (Summer 1988), which analyzes the opinion from the perspective of citizen responsibility in a democracy. Ashutosh A. Bhagwat, "The Story of *Whitney v. California*: The Power of Ideas," in Michael C. Dorf, *Constitutional Law Stories* (Eagan, MN: Foundation Press, 2009) traces the impact of the Brandeis concurrence on American law. Bradley C. Bobertz, "The Brandeis Gambit: The Making of America's 'First Freedom,' 1909–1931," 40 *William and Mary Law Review* 557 (1998–1999) and Stephen A. Smith, "Whitney v. California," in *Free Speech on Trial: Communication Perspectives on Landmark Supreme Court Decisions*, ed. Richard A. Parker (Tuscaloosa: University of Alabama Press, 2003) are among the other good articles about *Whitney*. For a less laudatory analysis, see Ronald K. L. Collins and David M. Skover's "Curious Concurrence: Justice Brandeis's Vote in Whitney v California," 2005 *Supreme Court Review* 333 (2005), which argues that Brandeis should have dissented rather than concurred in *Whitney*.

Brandeis's drafts in *Ruthenberg* and *Whitney*, along with correspondence about them, are housed at the Harvard Law School library (Louis D. Brandeis Papers, 1881–1996, box 44, folders 5–11). They can also be seen at http://pds.lib.harvard.edu/pds/view/14737316, and the library is willing to send them as PDFs, but unfortunately the pages in both versions are somewhat truncated. Go to http://www.firstamendmentcenter.org/madison/wp-content/uploads/2011/10/Brandeis_dissent_Ruthenberg.pdf for what is probably the final draft of the *Ruthenberg* dissent.

Information about Ruthenberg's life and works is in the very sympathetic Oakley C. Johnson, *The Day Is Coming: Life and Work of Charles E. Ruthenberg, 1882–1927* (New York: International Publishers, 1957), and Charles E. Ruthenberg, *Speeches and Writings of Charles E. Ruthenberg*, which contains an equally admiring short biographical introduction by Jay Lovestone (New York: International Publishers, 1928).

The papers of John Francis Neylan, who came into the *Whitney* case at the appeals level, are housed at the University of California–Berkeley's Bancroft

Library. The collection has folders relating to *Whitney*, including correspondence between Whitney and Neylan. Neylan Papers, BANC MSS C-B881. There is a Finding Aid at http://www.oac.cdlib.org/findaid/ark:/13030 /tf6q2n97zs/entire_text/. Neylan described Whitney and her case in a 1954 interview: *Politics, Law, and the University of California: An Interview Conducted by Dr. Corinne L. Gilb and Professor Walton E. Bean* (Berkeley: University of California, 1961), 133–143. Roger W. Lotchin, "John Francis Neylan: San Francisco Irish Progressive," in *The San Francisco Irish: 1850–1976*, ed. James P. Walsh (San Francisco: Irish Literary and Historical Society, 1978) has biographical information.

Similar information about Walter Nelles, one of the two ACLU lawyers at the Supreme Court level, is in "Walter Nelles," *Nellis News* 31, no. 1 (Summer 2001): 1. Louis H. Pollak, "Advocating Civil Liberties: A Young Lawyer before the Old Court," 17 *Harvard Civil Rights–Civil Liberties Law Review* 1 (Spring 1982) is an essay about Walter Pollak, the second ACLU attorney in the case, by Pollak's son, himself a civil rights lawyer, law school dean, and federal district court judge.

Information about the criminal syndicalism law at the heart of the *Whitney* case is in Stephen Rohde, "Criminal Syndicalism," 3 *Western Legal History* 309 (Summer/Fall 1990); George W. Kirchwey, *A Survey of the Workings of the Criminal Syndicalism Law of California* (California Committee, American Civil Liberties Union, 1926); and Eldridge Foster Dowell, *A History of Criminal Syndicalism Legislation in the United States* (Baltimore, MD: Johns Hopkins Press, 1939). The Dowell book includes a section on repeal efforts in California.

ACLU

The leading volume on the history of the ACLU is Samuel Walker, *In Defense of American Liberties: A History of the ACLU* (Oxford: Oxford University Press, 1990). Donald Johnson, *The Challenge to American Freedoms: World War I and the Rise of the American Civil Liberties Union* (Lexington: University of Kentucky Press, 1963) is an earlier work on the subject. David M. Rabban's "The Free Speech League, the ACLU, and Changing Conceptions of Free Speech in American History," mentioned above in the section on the First Amendment, places the ACLU in the context of earlier and later ideas about speech.

Roger Baldwin's life is covered in Peggy Lamson, *Roger Baldwin: Founder of the American Civil Liberties Union* (New York: Houghton Mifflin Co., 1976) and Robert Cottrell, *Roger Nash Baldwin and the American Civil Liberties Union* (New York: Columbia University Press, 2000). Part of a 1920 FBI report on "Roger Baldwin and the American Civil Liberties Union" is at http://www.marxist history.org/history/usa/groups/aclu/1920/0503-speer-onbaldwin.pdf. Baldwin's papers are at Princeton University's Mudd Library: http://findingaids .princeton.edu/collections/MC005. There is some information about Crystal

Eastman on the website of the National Women's Hall of Fame, http://www
.greatwomen.org/component/fabrik/details/2/55 and on the ACLU's site at
https://www.aclu.org/womens-rights/crystal-eastman.
The records of the Garland Fund are in the New York Public Library:
American Fund for Public Service, Records, 1922–1941, MssCol74. Gloria Gar-
rett Samson, *The American Fund for Public Service: Charles Garland and Radical
Philanthropy, 1922–1941* (Westport, CT: Greenwood Press, 1996) tells the story of
the Fund. Walter Nelles, *A Liberal in Wartime: The Education of Albert DeSilver*
(New York: W. W. Norton & Co., 1940), chs. 6 and 7, provides an insider's view
of the National Civil Liberties Bureau and the young ACLU during World
War I and immediately thereafter. Records detailing the ACLU's efforts in the
Whitney case and its campaign to undo criminal syndicalism laws are housed
in Princeton University's Seeley G. Mudd Manuscript Library, American
Civil Liberties Union Records: MC001.03, MC001.03.02, Box 2905 & MC001.01,
Volumes 324, 324, and 351.

Critiques of First Amendment Jurisprudence

Some of the leading works by Critical Legal Studies scholars are Mari Mat-
suda, Charles R. Lawrence III, Richard Delgado, and Kimberlé Williams
Crenshaw, *Words That Wound: Critical Race Theory, Assaultive Speech, and the First
Amendment* (Boulder, CO: Westview Press, 1993); Duncan Kennedy, *Legal Edu-
cation and the Reproduction of Hierarchy: A Polemic against the System* (New York:
New York University Press, 2004); Richard Delgado, "*Words That Wound: A
Tort Action for Racial Insults, Epithets, and Name-Calling,*" 17 *Harvard Civil Rights–
Civil Liberties Law Review* 133 (1982); Charles R. Lawrence III, "*If He Hollers Let
Him Go: Regulating Racist Speech on Campus,*" 1990 *Duke Law Journal* 431 (1990); and
Mari Matsuda, "*Public Response to Racist Speech: Considering the Victim's Story,*" 87
Michigan Law Review 2320 (1989). Catharine A. MacKinnon, *Toward a Feminist
Theory of the State* (1989); MacKinnon, *Only Words* (1993); and MacKinnon, *Wom-
en's Lives, Men's Laws* (2005), all published by the Harvard University Press,
are among that author's works, and are complemented by Andrea Dworkin,
Pornography: Men Possessing Women (New York: E. P. Dutton, 1989).
William B. Fisch, "Hate Speech in the Constitutional Law of the United
States," 50 *American Journal of Comparative Law* 463 (Autumn 2002), is an anal-
ysis of the Supreme Court's decisions on the subject of hate speech. Kenneth
D. Ward, "Free Speech and the Development of Liberal Virtues: An Exam-
ination of the Controversies Involving Flag-Burning and Hate Speech," 52
University of Miami Law Review 733 (1997–1998) suggests there can be restrictions
on hate speech without harming the First Amendment. Robert C. Post, "Racist Speech, Democracy, and the First Amendment," 32 *William & Mary Law
Review* 267 (1990–1991) presents the opposing point of view, suggesting that

any such restrictions may harm democratic self-government and therefore should be carefully thought through. Jeremy Waldron, *The Harm in Hate Speech* (Cambridge, MA: Harvard University Press, 2012) argues that hate speech is harmful and advocates state regulation of group libel. Former Supreme Court Justice John Paul Stevens critiqued Waldron's book in "Should Hate Speech Be Outlawed?," *New York Review of Books*, June 7, 2012, http://www.nybooks.com/articles/archives/2012/jun/07/should-hate-speech-be-outlawed/.

Danielle Keats Citron, *Hate Crimes in Cyberspace* (Cambridge, MA: Harvard University Press, 2014), surveys existing laws that can be used to punish Internet hate speech and suggests possible additions. Martha C. Nussbaum, "Haterz Gonna Hate?," *Nation*, November 24, 2014, 28–33, is an interesting essay about the Citron book and the subject, suggesting a closer examination of the societal forces that lead to some Internet hate speech.

Gabriel Weimann, "www.terror.net: How Modern Terrorism Uses the Internet," United States Institute of Peace Special Report 116 (March 2004), available at http://www.usip.org/sites/default/files/sr116.pdf, examines that subject. For a discussion of how to guard against terrorists' use of the Internet while safeguarding free speech and other civil liberties, see John D. Podesta and Raj Goyle, "Lost in Cyberspace? Finding American Liberties in a Dangerous Digital World," 23 *Yale Law & Policy Review* 509 (2005), available at http://cdn.americanprogress.org/wp-content/uploads/kf/PODESTA_GOYLE_070105.PDF. Chris Montgomery, "Can *Brandenburg v. Ohio* Survive the Internet and the Age of Terrorism?: The Secret Weakening of a Venerable Doctrine," 70 *Ohio State Law Journal* 141 (2009) examines U.S. government attempts to suppress terrorist speech without implicating the First Amendment, by encouraging Internet service providers to censor such speech.

Mark A. Graber, *Transforming Free Speech: The Ambiguous Legacy of Civil Libertarianism* (Oakland: University of California Press, 1991) criticizes the theories of Chafee and others for ignoring the economic component that he argues makes it difficult if not impossible for some speech to be heard, and attacks the Supreme Court's rulings that monetary contributions to political campaigns are the equivalent of speech.

The quotes in chapter 7 about American hysteria are from Richard Hofstadter, "The Paranoid Style in American Politics," *Harper's Magazine*, November, 1964, 77–86, available at http://harpers.org/archive/1964/11/the-paranoid-style-in-american-politics/; Anthony Lewis, *Freedom for the Thought That We Hate*, cited above in the section on the First Amendment, 21; and Frank Bruni, "Scarier Than Ebola," *New York Times*, October 15, 2014, A31 c.1. The review of Chafee's *Freedom of Speech* quoted in that chapter is Thomas Reed Powell, "The American Inquisition," *Nation*, March 9, 1921, 377–379, at 378.

Free Speech Jurisprudence Abroad

The decision in *Canada (Human Rights Comm.) v. Taylor*, the Canadian case discussed in chapter 7, is at http://scc-csc.lexum.com/scc-csc/scc-csc/en/item /697/index.do. The Skokie case is recounted in Philippa Strum, *When the Nazis Came to Skokie: Freedom for the Speech We Hate* (Lawrence: University Press of Kansas, 1999).

Laws against hate speech in most countries can be found by searching on the Web for the name of the country and "speech" or "constitution." The website LegislationLine has a list, with links, of the criminal codes of many countries. http://www.legislationline.org/documents/section/criminal-codes. Go to the links and search for "speech," "race," and/or "religion." The Council of Europe website, http://www.coe.int/t/dghl/monitoring/ecri/legal_research /national_legal_measures/, lists hate speech laws of the countries on that continent, with links. Michel Rosenfeld, "Hate Speech in Constitutional Jurisprudence: A Comparative Analysis" (James Burns Institute for Advanced Legal Studies, Working Paper Series No. 41, April 2001) also examines laws of European countries. http://www.law.ox.ac.uk/news/events_files/2012_- _LRC_Hate_Speech_Memorandum.pdf. "Comparative Hate Speech Laws: A Memorandum," written by Oxford University faculty and students and prepared for the Legal Resources Centre, South Africa (March 2012), is an interesting comparison of such laws in a number of countries. http://www.law .ox.ac.uk/news/events_files/2012_-_LRC_Hate_Speech_Memorandum.pdf. Ivan Hare and James Weinstein, eds., *Extreme Speech and Democracy* (Oxford: Oxford University Press, 2009), includes essays about speech laws in many nations as well as a discussion of religious, gender, and homophobic hate speech.

The International Covenant on Civil and Political Rights Convention is at http://www.ohchr.org/en/professionalinterest/pages/ccpr.aspx; the International Convention on the Elimination of All Forms of Racial Discrimination, at http://www.ohchr.org/EN/ProfessionalInterest/Pages/CERD.aspx. Ivan Hare, "Extreme Speech under International and Regional Human Rights Standards," in Hare and Weinstein, *Extreme Speech and Democracy*, mentioned above, is a synopsis of international and regional (primarily European) human rights instruments relating to speech.

INDEX